SERVING READERS

Edited by Ted Balcom

FOR THE
Illinois Library Association

HIGHSMITH PRESS HANDBOOK SERIES

Fort Atkinson, Wisconsin

Published by Highsmith Press LLC
W5527 Highway 106
P.O. Box 800
Fort Atkinson, Wisconsin 53538-0800
1-800-558-2110

© Illinois Library Association, 1997
Cover by Mary Ann Highsmith

The paper used in this publication meets the minimum requirements of
American National Standard for Information Science —
Permanence of Paper for Printed Library Material. ANSI/NISO Z39.48-1984.

Library of Congress Cataloging-in-Publication Data

Serving readers / edited by Ted Balcom, for the Illinois
    Library Association.
        p.   cm. –(Highsmith Press handbook series)
    Includes bibliographical references and index.
    ISBN 0-917846-74-5 (alk. paper)
    1. Reader guidance–United States. I. Balcom, Ted.
II. Illinois Library Association. III. Series.
Z711.4.S48 1997
025.5'4–DC20   96-38513
                                                         CIP

ISBN 0-917846-74-5

Contents

Introduction

Ted Balcom

Serving Readers seems to me just the right title for this timely and much-needed book, which brings together a collection of presentations developed to provide guidance in the area of readers' advisory service. After all, "serving readers" is a large part of every librarian's job—many would say, the most important part. Yet it is an activity about which not nearly enough has been written, and librarians who are interested in building their skills in the critical area of serving readers at the readers' advisory desk can find very little information in either books or journals to support their desire to improve their skills.

It is because of this unfortunate paucity of relevant information that in Illinois, several groups of librarians have formed over the last ten years, committed to developing continuing education activities that do speak to their goal of becoming better readers' advisors. These librarians were frustrated with conference schedules that promoted programs about online searching, automated circulation systems, CD-ROM reference tools and other forms of technology, but never gave support to the effort of leading readers toward books they might enjoy. Tired of suggesting ideas for programs that were never offered, they decided to strike out on their own and organize the kind of continuing education opportunities they had been craving—and knew others in the profession would respond to positively, as well.

Thus was born the Adult Reading Round Table, followed by the Mid-Illinois Readers' Advisory Group and the DuPage Library System Readers' Advisory Special Interest Group. All of these organizations explored the topic of readers' advisory from various perspectives—from writing bibliographies and setting up displays to leading book discussions and studying genre fiction. Out of the programs that these groups successfully presented over a period of years came a special track of readers' advisory skill-building programs at the 1995 Illinois Library Association Conference, held in Peoria, Illinois. Donald Sager, of Highsmith Press, was the co-chair of that conference, and it was his worthwhile idea to publish the text of those readers' advisory programs, in order to bring their valuable concepts to a wider audience.

And so, gathered together in this book, you will find the information about serving readers that was shared in various meeting rooms in Peoria. In most cases, these talks had been presented first for other groups, and were being repeated, with some updating, for the ILA audience. In order to make them read more smoothly as essays for this book, some revising and editing were necessary. But what emerges now on the printed page is true to the spirit of the original presentations, giving the librarian who wishes to improve his or her readers' advisory skills a great deal of meaningful and stimulating advice. Not every piece will speak to the need of every readers' advisor, but there is in this collection such a variety of interesting viewpoints and such a depth of practical knowledge, that there is bound to be something new to be discovered, something useful to be learned, something provocative to be considered.

If readers' advisory is a new concept to you, this helpful book will open your eyes to easy but effective ways to connect your patrons with titles they are sure to enjoy. You will learn the important role that genre study plays in developing a skilled readers' advisor. The book provides useful examples of genre study as well, focussing closely on such popular genres as historical fiction and fantasy fiction. Also explored is the development of readers' advisory service to meet the needs of specific segments of the public library's clientele—children and men. And the value of a well-managed fiction collection in supporting high-quality readers' advisory service is examined in depth.

Librarians who have chosen (or who have been assigned) to do readers' advisory work usually feel blessed—they end up loving what they do. It is gratifying work, because it results in giving the library user exactly what he or she wants, and the user ultimately feels very positive about the library experience. But in addition to the wonderful payoff of user satisfaction, there is also the important factor that real library skills are demanded—skills that few others, besides librarians, have—and those are skills that are enjoyable to develop and to use. All that has been missing is that there are few good resources available to help the readers' advisor reach out and become even better at the job. Now, with *Serving Readers*, it is hoped that to some significant degree, that gap has been filled.

First, You Read

Chapter One

Ted Balcom

During the past ten years in library circles, there has been a marked resurgence of interest in readers' advisory service. At the beginning of this trend, many librarians weren't sure what all the clamor was about. They found themselves asking skeptically, "Just exactly what is this readers' advisory service, and why should my library take time and spend money to provide it?"

Supporters of readers' advisory quickly came forward to offer a clear definition of the service and to demonstrate its value. Books and articles on the subject began to appear, and workshops were presented. Librarians did their homework and started to formulate service programs for their clientele.

Over time, a particular aspect of readers' advisory training has emerged as the key to strengthening the service. That aspect is genre study.

In this chapter, I'm going to explain why genre study is so important to the development of high quality readers' advisory skills.

Everyone likes "read-alikes"

I believe the connection lies in the public's strong interest in "read-alikes." I'm fairly certain that most readers know what a "read-alike" is, but just in case, let me offer some clarification. Readers discover an author that they like. Then they tend to read all of that author's works. When they're finished, they want to read something similar. What they're looking for is a "read-alike." But often they don't know where to look for a "read-alike" on their own. "Read-alikes" are not grouped together in the library collection or the catalog. The closest kind of assistance provided in this regard is the genre collection, and not all libraries separate their fiction collection into genres. And so, the reader comes to the librarian for help. This means that the librarian has to be an expert on genres. Who writes in which genre? What are the qualities of a specific genre? Which writers write alike? And what does the library own—and what's available?

It's a lot to know and remember. But it's information that patrons want. It's what helps them to use the library collection and to get the most out of it. And that's why it's important.

Readers prefer genres

Most librarians are aware that their patrons read in genres. This is what they, also, like to do. Readers are generally unwilling to cross over into other genres. This is even true of librarians as readers! This is one of the hurdles that librarians have to overcome when they embark on genre study. They have to start reading books that they wouldn't ordinarily pick for themselves, and they have to read a lot of these books. They have to become familiar with the books—the authors and the way they write—and why readers like them. They have to find the connection between certain authors—and to remember those connections. This is what genre study is all about.

One of the reasons that patrons like fiction collections organized by genre is because this organization helps them to find what they like to read more quickly. It helps them to identify a book they will be interested in reading—without careful examination.

Genre collections help the librarian, too. During the readers' advisory interview, the librarian has a limited amount of time to connect the reader with a book. The readers' advisor is really trying to make a sale—and send that reader out of the library with a book under his or her arm, a book that the reader has a good chance of enjoying. In order to make that sale, the librarian has to know the merchandise. And that's why we have to study genres and get to know them as well as we can.

Many of you are familiar with the Adult Reading Round Table (ARRT), an organization of librarians in the Chicagoland area that has been providing readers' advisory workshops for the past ten years. About four years ago, when I was a member of the ARRT Steering Committee, I proposed the formation of a genre study group. I had two aims in mind: one was to create an opportunity for ARRT members, myself included, to learn more about specific genres and the other was to develop a model for learning that other groups could adopt.

Forming a genre study group

When the ARRT Genre Study Group began, we didn't know exactly how we wanted to go about achieving our purpose. But we decided a good way to start was to pick a genre that most of us knew little about. We chose science fiction. None of us read it of our own accord, but we all agreed that we needed to know more about it in order to better serve our patrons.

In retrospect, I think we were half-right. I think it is valid to pick a genre you don't know and also one that is popular in your community. That makes it important for you to be knowledgeable about that genre. But I also think it is very hard for you to learn about a genre when no one in the group knows anything about it. It is hard to know just where to go when no one has been there before. So, there is value in finding an expert who will participate with you, someone who can steer you in the right direction. This will save you a lot of time.

Discovering subgenres

With the ARRT group, we sort of figured it out as we went along. With science fiction, we thought our biggest challenge was going to be identifying the difference between pure science fiction and fantasy. Then, as we got into our study, we began to discover the amazing spectrum of science fiction, with "hard" science fiction at one end, and "soft" science fiction at the other, plus all the subgenres! Invaders from outer space... time travel... end-of-the-world adventures... alternate worlds... space explorers... cyberpunk... and on and on.

Find an expert in your chosen genre

An expert in your group can really help to chart the path of study—who you should read and how various authors connect, also providing interesting background information about the books and authors in the genre.

If you don't have an expert to draw upon, perhaps your group leader or leaders should take the time to do some research and draw up at least a partial syllabus before you get started, so that you do have a direction and everyone knows what it is.

One thing—if you don't dip into a genre, you don't realize that so many sub-genres even exist! You begin to see that science fiction readers, for example, may like some subgenres, but not others, which is why you, as the readers' advisor, need to be knowledgeable about the differences.

You can't just point them in the direction of the science fiction books or rec-ommend Robert Heinlein, Isaac Asimov, and Arthur C. Clarke and let it go at that!

The value of working with a group

If you are going to get involved in genre study, I think the best way to do it is with a group. A group gives you the value of discussion—you can learn so much from the insights of others! In the process, your own opinions and conclusions may be challenged, opening up new perspectives.

There are several ways you can go:

* you can form a group within a library department
* within a library staff
* among representatives from several libraries
* or even with a number of friends.

As you form your group, you will need to decide:

1. How often will you meet?

   Consider—once a month, or every other month. Your schedule will deter-mine how much you read between sessions. What is realistic?

2. How long will the sessions run?
   At least two hours? How much time do you have to meet?

3. How long will you study one genre?
   A year? Two years?

4. How will you know when you're done?
   Maybe you're never really done, but at some point, you will feel like you've done enough, that you now have a better feel for the genre, and you're ready to go on to something else. There is a tendency to burn out in genre study, particularly if you are reading a lot of the same kind of books and they are not the sort of books that you especially like. Of course, the level of burn-out varies from reader to reader and can be different from one genre to another.

And first of all, you must read

You must make the commitment to read… and then read more. This is very important. If you don't to take the time to read, you will be tempted to stop par-ticipating and therefore, stop learning.

How much to read?

So that leads into your decision on how much to read. With ARRT, we decided first to read two books for each discussion and then moved the number up to three, in order to cover more ground.

Who will decide what the group is to read? Naturally, the whole group wants to be included in this decision, but there is again the value of an expert, who can guide you to the important works in a genre.

Be aware that group members will have different levels of knowledgeability. And in your sessions, you must be careful not to end up spending a lot of time dis-cussing what to read next, since this takes time away from the time you have to dis-cuss what you have already read.

Even if you can't form a group, it's probably a good idea to at least find a genre study partner, one other person who will share this undertaking with you. You can keep each other com-mitted to the project and focused on what you are trying to accomplish. Alone, it's too easy to slip off the track, and I think you need that validation that comes from sharing your responses with someone else and get-ting their feedback.

Important organizational factors to consider:

The need for a leader: Someone to guide the dis-cussions, to get everyone to participate, to draw a con-sensus at the end of the dis-cussion.

The need for a notetaker: Someone to put down the highlights of the discussion (often hard to pick out as they are occurring), some-one to provide a record for those who miss the meet-ing, also to note what has been accomplished, what the group has uncovered in its study and now better understands. The notetaker needs to look for "little ker-nels of truth" in the discus-sion—perhaps the leader can help to pick these out.

Consider rotating these jobs, to keep the group members more interested in the discussions.

One good place to start: refer to Betty Rosenberg's *Genreflecting* and other books or articles about the genre. Start out by looking for "benchmark" authors. A benchmark author is one who is an especially skilled practitioner of the genre, popular and critically acclaimed. Other writers are often compared to such an author, to determine if their achievement meets the same standard. The value of reading benchmark authors is that this grounds you in the genre, giving you a sense of its primary characteristics and why readers enjoy it. It also helps for you to become familiar with benchmark authors so that you can talk about them with readers. It gives you a jumping off place for your conversations about the genre.

As you read more in the genre, you can use these benchmark writers in making comparisons with other authors, particularly newcomers to the field. For example, if you know what Agatha Christie is like, you can see ways that P.D. James is like her and ways that they are different. You have to determine with your patron—Are the qualities she likes in Agatha Christie also present in a writer like P.D. James? If she likes James, will she also like Martha Grimes and Ruth Rendell? In reading Ruth Rendell, you may discover that she publishes under a pseudonym as well—Barbara Vine. How are the Vine books different from those written as Rendell? Can you recommend all of these books to the same reader?

Two types of discussions

In a genre study group, there can be two types of discussions: one, where everyone reads the same book, and the other, where everyone reads a different book (their own selection) or books by different authors, with similar themes.

When everyone reads the same book, you can get into more depth in your discussion, because everyone has common ground.

With different books, there's the benefit of exposure to more titles, but you may not find out as much about the book because each member is making a brief report. And the person making the report may not grasp the most important aspects of the book. Finally, the book may not stick with you because you didn't actually read it yourself.

Perhaps you should try it both ways, and see what works best for your group.

What will you look for in your reading?

First of all, don't assume that everyone in the group has some familiarity with the benchmark authors in the genre you've chosen to study. Just as not everyone reads in all genres, some people don't know anything about certain prominent authors, even though they can correctly associate them with the genres in which they write. They've heard of them, but they don't really know how they write. This is really the whole point of genre study. If you've never read a Danielle Steel novel, how can you explain the appeal of her work—and how can you guide a reader to other similar books?

Look for the appeal of the genre

Now here is the most important thing you do in genre study. You look for the appeal of the genre as a whole—and for the special appeal of certain authors and certain books.

You can define the appeal by focusing on various characteristics of the book, asking yourself certain questions about the book. Every book in the genre has certain similar characteristics. Those characteristics are what the reader looks for when considering whether or not to read a particular book; or if he has indeed made the decision to read the book, whether or not that book turns out to be a satisfying genre-reading experience. I think this survey of characteristics is almost a sub-conscious process on the part of the reader.

How the author handles these characteristics is important for you to be aware of as you study the book. You must look for what's there—and what isn't. You don't need to be making judgments about how well it's done. You're just trying to determine if the necessary elements are there for a potential reader to enjoy. Then you are comparing this work with the accomplishment of a benchmark author.

Ask yourself: How does this author—and this particular book—fit in to the genre?

What readers look for

I think there are some specific factors that most readers look for when considering whether a book is worth reading. They are:

- **Protagonist**—male or female?
- **Time period**—contemporary or historical?
- **Setting**—domestic or foreign?
- **Social class of the characters**—rich or poor… or somewhere in between?
- **Density of the story**— How big is the book? Are there lots of details and description—or is it sparsely written?
- **Pacing and action**—How fast does the book move? Is it a "page-turner"?
- **Conflict**— Finally, probably the most important factor: What is the dramatic hook? What's the conflict in the story?

The reader's response to these factors may vary, depending upon mood, but basically, these are the things that readers want to know in making their choices. They are also the characteristics that you should look for when engaging in genre study. How are these factors handled within the genre, and how are they handled within a specific book?

Protagonist… time period… setting… social class of the characters… density of the story… pace… and dramatic hook.

Other qualities will influence the reader's enjoyment of the tale: how the characters are developed, the author's style, plausibility of the plot and so on.

Questions to keep in mind when studying books and working with readers

Here are some other things to think about as you do your reading and prepare to discuss the books you've read with other members of your group.

- Does the book emphasize plot over character—or is it a good combination of both?
- Is the plot simple and predictable—or complex, full of interesting twists and turns?
- Is it a formula plot? (You must realize that some readers really want this.) Or does it fall in between—not too simplistic, not too challenging.
- Look at the characters. Are they stereotypes, or are they fresh and original? Are they people the reader can care about, people with depth, with human frailties?
- Does the story contain interesting supporting characters?
- Think about the relationships between the characters. Are they well developed?
- Are there subplots? Do they add texture—or confusion?

In successful genre study you must see and think about—
What's included
How it's presented
How satisfying will it be to fans of the genre?

- Be aware of the author's style—is it simple and straight forward, or elegant and mannered? How will this affect the potential reader?

- Think about the author's intent: Is it to entertain? To teach? To comment?

Some readers want a message

- Is there a message to the story? Some readers want this, others don't. And sometimes it works, and sometimes it doesn't. It may be all in the way it's handled.

- What is the point of view? Is there a first person narrator? First person can really pull the reader into the story, but what does the reader like? Does it make a difference?

- What are the themes in the story? Some you may find intriguing, others you may find disturbing. Some readers like dark themes or stories with hard edges.

- What is the tone of the book? Is it heavy or light? Pessimistic or optimistic? Realistic or fantastic? All of this will make a difference to the book's potential reader.

- Does the book have an emotional impact? This may not be a requirement for all readers, but some are looking for novels with a strong effect.

- To what extent are ingredients like romance, suspense, action, violence, and sex included—and emphasized? Does the book have touches of humor? Is there any quirkiness or offbeat quality? Sometimes that's exactly what the reader will ask for. The appeal of the book has to relate to the reader's mood.

- Are there any qualities that might put the reader off? For example, dialect can be annoying to some readers, especially if it's overused. What about foreign names? Are there a lot of them that seem similar, and could therefore be confusing? How about a lot of technological jargon? These kinds of elements can persuade a reader to put the book down—and never pick it up again.

- What is the flavor of the book? Does it have a particular mood about it?

- Are you and the author on the same wave length? Can you get comfortable with this book? Or is getting comfortable not really the issue with this title?

- Would you read other books by this author? Other books similar to this one?

- Does the book have a sort of cinematic quality to it that might help to describe its appeal to a patron? For example, does it remind you of Hitchcock? *Star Wars*? John Wayne? These days, everyone is so attuned to popular culture that this may be an effective way for you to "sell" the book to a patron.

Using what you've learned

How do you use what you have learned in genre study? By knowing the characteristics of books in a genre, you know what to look for when you read. In the readers' advisory interview, you find out how the reader reacts to these qualities, and then you go about selecting an appropriate book for the reader, based on your knowledge of books and your awareness of what the reader says he likes.

As you read, you will become increasingly aware of the existence of subgenres and overlapping genres. Sometimes the line between genres can be rather blurry. For instance, the line between science fiction and fantasy—or the line between mystery and horror. It's important to be aware of the differences in similar or related genres, since readers can become very upset when they're expecting one type of story and you hand them another.

Genre book clubs are constantly being marketed to readers through maga-

As readers' advisers, we have to know which books to look for and recommend, even if they don't suit our personal tastes.

Readers like series

Remember that people like to read books in series, not only other books by the same author, but books that feature the same character. This is such a strong phenomenon that some beloved characters haven't died when their authors did. For instance, Nero Wolfe, James Bond, Scarlett O'Hara and Mrs. DeWinter are still having new adventures, even though their creators are no longer with us.

The core of readers' advisory service:

You read; you think about what you read; you remember. Then you find out what the reader enjoys, and you select an appropriate book for the reader, based on your knowledge of books and your awareness of what the reader says he likes.

zines and newspapers. Publishers have long known about the interest in genre reading, and they capitalize on it. One of the interesting things that librarians can learn from this is that the book clubs include mainstream authors in with the genre selections. For instance, the Mystery Guild throws Jeffrey Archer in with John Grisham, and Mary Higgins Clark in with Dominick Dunne. They're not exactly "read-alikes," but there may be enough similarity in some of their themes to attract some readers who are willing to cross over. And from Dominick Dunne, they may be willing to jump to a nonfiction true crime writer like Ann Rule. Observing this kind of phenomenon as part of your study is another way of expanding your knowledge about what constitutes a genre and what you can recommend to readers.

Genre study tips

Short stories and genre magazines: Consider reading some short stories. Also, look at special genre magazines (your readers do!) such as *Romantic Times* and *The Armchair Detective.* Read articles about genres in the mass media, as well as in library publications. Check Info Trac and the *Reader's Guide* under the genre name.

Books and book reviews about the genre: Peruse books about the genre— look in your library's catalog for ideas. Another source of information—book reviews. Selectors, read beyond your own area of selection, to be aware of what's new and liable to become hot. Listen to audiobooks if you're in the car a lot—the abridged versions are a great way to sample a wealth of different authors. Don't forget reference books! The annual volume of *Contemporary Authors* has wonderful information about notable writers of the year.

Remember what you read and take notes: As you work through your study, make the commitment to remember what you're learning. Perhaps that means making lists and notes or some kind of card files to refer to, now and then. Develop bibliographies and displays that are genre-related—put what you've learned to use.

Talk to others about what you're reading: I must stress the importance of talking about your genre reading with others, even outside your study group. You can learn a lot from patrons, colleagues, friends, and relatives.

There may be someone on your staff who has special expertise in regard to a genre, someone who doesn't work as a readers' advisor, like a cataloger or a page— be willing to try to tap that resource! You may learn unexpected new things about the genre you're studying, you may get valuable reading suggestions, and you will be sharing as a staff.

The fun of identifying new genres

Our genre study group has had fun identifying new genres—before they appear in the textbooks. We watched—and read—with interest as Tom Clancy blazed the trail to techno-thrillers; Robert James Waller rediscovered middle-aged romance; and Thomas Harris kicked off the craze for serial killers.

You'll need to look for something we call "gentle" reads, too, with no graphic sex or violence, and a warm, upbeat ending. You'll find new examples of good old-fashioned storytellers, who combine engaging characters and enthralling plots. Be on the look-out for novels about relationships (families and others) and for "women's fiction"—which is different from romance.

Which genres are most popular in your library? You should know this. Make a list. Get other staff members to help you, and share the information.

And why do I say, "First, you read?" Because you must do quite a bit of reading before you can start drawing conclusions. You have to know what exists, what it's *really* like, and how the books differ from one another. So reading is very important. You must read to discover the appeal. Remember, you are trying to see the books in comparison to each other. Is this one more like A—or B? Is it "hard" or "soft" —or somewhere in between? Where does it fit in to the genre?

You don't have to like it

And as you read more, you will start thinking about how effective the book is—is it good of its type? Does it succeed on its own terms? It's not so much whether you liked it, but will the reader who likes this genre like it?

In the study group, you do end up talking a lot about what you liked and what you didn't—this seems unavoidable where librarians are involved—but in the end the discussion does have to come back to whether or not the book is worth recommending, and therefore, worth remembering.

Again, always ask yourself, will your reader be likely to enjoy it? We've had many great discussions in our group, with lots of disagreements based on personal responses. But always be aware of the difference between liking a genre and knowing about it.

Another challenge: Eventually you will want to recommend genre books to someone who usually doesn't read in that genre. You'll be introducing new readers to a genre based on what you think they'll enjoy.

The ultimate pay-off is the more genre study you do, the more you will build your confidence as a readers' advisor. Skill-building is something we all need to do, in order to improve. It's hard work, but it's worth the effort. I urge you to give it a try!

A caution: There's the danger of confronting too many possibilities. Know from the beginning that you don't have to read everything. Your goal is to become more knowledgeable, not to become a total expert. You want to know more, so you can be more helpful, that's all.

Managing Fiction Collections

Chapter Two

Georgine N. Olson

Libraries invest too much in the way of personnel and financial resources in their fiction collections not to be as thoughtful about the development of their fiction collections as they are about the development of their nonfiction and reference collections. Yet many a library *grows* its fiction collection based on hunches and instinct rather than *developing* the collection based on knowledge and data.

This chapter is an introduction to a more "scientific" management of fiction collections. It will present a variety of ways to study your collection and its use, and it will present some tools to help you formulate decisions about the fiction collection that are best for your library. The goal is to give you a different perspective, a new way of thinking about how best to manage your library's fiction collection.

All libraries are different—all patron groups are different—all staff are different. As with so much else in the field of librarianship, there is no simple, one-size-fits-all method to follow. However, I can provide you with several tools from which you can choose those that best suit your library's needs.

The Great Wheel

Several of the world's religions view life as a great wheel; scientists write about life cycles. I don't think I'd go as far as to claim that managing fiction collections is either a religious or a scientific experience. However, I do find it helpful to think of collection management as a wheel, a cycle, a circle. You start with the library's mission and long-range plan. This leads to a collection management plan. This has an effect on how you establish a materials budget. The budget effects selection and acquisition. Then you assess or study the collection and its use. This generally leads to weeding and some redirection of selection and acquisition policies. Then you seek community input or community analysis, which brings you back to a review of your mission statement and long range plan. This leads to a review of your collection management plan. And so the wheel spins...

We are quite used to this type of cycle for nonfiction, but it works equally well and is equally important for fiction collections. Given the use of and demand for popular reading materials in our libraries, there is ample reason for fiction collections to be carefully managed and reviewed to insure that they satisfactorily meet the needs of the community.

Think of collection management as a wheel, a cycle, a circle.

Collection management plans

Take a moment to reflect on your library's collection management plans as they now exist and then think about how you would answer the following questions:

1. Would a stranger, a member of the public, a board member, or a member of the city council be able to read your fiction collection management plan or policies and understand what you do—and why it is done that way?

2. Does the library list its selection criteria? Are the criteria reflective of the library's stated goals and backed by a clear knowledge of what your patrons want?

3. Is there a section on weeding/deaccession that specifically addresses how both classic and popular fiction items are weeded (or how you identify a title as "classic"), or how to weed based on use, or how to weed based on shelf space? After all, space is finite, and it would be a good idea for libraries to address space constraints in their collection development policies.

4. Does the fiction collection development policy explain how the library handles gifts, memorials, or bequests?

5. Does the collection policy address items either long overdue or lost due to theft? Why and/or when should a library replace titles that are always "disappearing"? Is there a difference between those that are controversial titles or those on student reading lists? It's frequently an ongoing battle to hang on to vulnerable titles (i.e. *Of Mice and Men*) that are regularly read by a wide variety of people. A library's collection management plan might state that it will strive to keep an equal number of copies in general circulation and on special reserve—and that it will purchase additional copies of titles that are more than X months overdue. Items that are in the collection but are not available are a common frustration to both librarians and patrons, one that should be addressed in collection management plans.

We all know libraries where it seems that the only way to add a new book is to discard an older one. Addressing space constraints in a collection management policy is not only a useful way to address chronic space needs, it can serve as a wake-up call to funders about the need for an addition or a new facility.

Budget allocations

It is interesting to note that a public library that has undertaken a planning and role setting exercise and selected popular materials center as a primary role, would, according to the suggested implementation of a primary role, put *80 percent* of its materials budget, into that primary role. True, if the library is a popular materials center and is expends 80 percent of the materials budget on popular materials, this could include home repair, gardening, cookery, movie star biographies, etc. as well as fiction. Well, then, what portion of that 80 percent of the budget would go towards the purchase of fiction as a major portion of what we classify as popular reading material?

Many of us would like guidelines in setting the library's budget for fiction. The procedures below can help you establish a fiction budget appropriate to suit your library.

1. Determine what percent of your total circulation is fiction. Include all formats and media that you consider to be fiction.

2. Multiply this percentage by your total materials budget.

3. Check recent invoices to find what your library has been paying for fiction and non-fiction. This will encompass your library's vendor discount and the mix of hardbacks, paperbacks, formats, and media that is unique to your library. Or—check the *Bowker Annual, Publishers Weekly* and/or *Library Journal* for their annual section on the price of library materials.

4. Subtract the basic cost of a fiction book from that of a non-fiction book. If the average fiction book is $15 and the average non-fiction book is $20, the average fiction book cost three-fourths as much as the average non-fiction book.

5. Now multiply the dollar amount from no. 2 times the percentage from no. 4 for a suggested baseline budget for fiction that is based on both use of the collection and the current cost of fiction titles.

If you are uncertain that the dollar amount reached by this method is appropriate, you might check the fiction budgets of similar sized libraries in your state. Library materials budgets are part of public library reports to most state libraries. Since this information is public knowledge, it's not hard to develop a list of libraries similar in size, serving similar communities, and then compare materials budgets. If your library spends $2,000 a year on fiction and 80 percent of your benchmark libraries spend $6,000, your library would seem to have a good case for increasing its fiction budget!

If, because it is old, or the library has not been selecting well, or the budget is recovering from tight times, the library's fiction circulation seems unusually low, a library might do well to try some other approaches to deciding how much to budget for fiction. It might be a good idea to identify libraries in the area or database that have good and/or well-circulating fiction collections—and use their budgets as benchmarks. Prior to acting on these budget comparisons, librarians would be wise to visit possible benchmark libraries to familiarize themselves with the libraries, their fiction collection and its use.

Fiction collection guidelines – size and content

It's not always easy to be confident that you are building the best fiction collection you can for your library. Quantitatively, there are many things to consider:

1. What size collection should I have?

2. What's a good guideline for the number of copies I should have of new, popular or classic titles?

3. Should I have books by all the major authors?

4. Should I have all the books by major authors?

5. What percentage of the authors should I have?

The *Hennepin County Collection Maintenance Manual* includes an interesting and useful set of guidelines that are fairly easy to work with. Hennepin County is a suburban Minneapolis library system that has libraries of several different sizes. The manual is pretty specific about the size and depth of fiction collections based on the size of the library and its community. It is not a bad starting point for those who would feel more comfortable with quantitative criteria.

Quality fiction

All else being equal, most librarians would feel a bit easier if they were assured that their patrons were insured access to "quality" fiction, whether the patrons chose to read it or not!

Many a library simply checks its collection against established lists of materials. If the library has a good percentage of the titles and authors listed, it can rest easy about the underlying "quality" of the collection. Wilson's *Fiction Catalog* presents a good, solid basic public library collection. A book like *Genreflecting* will help a library decide if its collection is representative across a genre. There are lists of "best new books" that are published each year—in *Library Journal*, in *Booklist*, and in other resources libraries regularly use. These lists can help libraries catch titles that really should have been purchased, but somehow just "slipped by."

In an LSCA-funded project involving ten small rural libraries in Central Illinois, some of the libraries used a title checklist, developed by the project consultant, which combined lists from a variety of resources. The libraries discovered, when they matched their fiction collections to these checklists and then compared the results with each other, that the concept of what constitutes a "quality" collection can be very different from library to library. The "quality" titles purchased for one community are not necessarily those selected for another—particularly in a library with a small collection. The fact is: the quality titles chosen by a small library are still a very small portion of what is published. Individually these libraries collect at a minimal level (important authors, core titles); together, because of different acquisition criteria, they can be equal to a good, mid-sized collection with supplementary titles and multiple copies of key popular titles. This finding provided impetus for some of the Illinois project libraries to join their regional database and to participate in cooperative collection management programs to enhance the resources available to each library's readers.

As a way to insure that a library's collection maintains a minimal level of "quality" fiction, a section in the library's collection management plan could state, "The library will purchase every book listed in the annual supplements to the *Fiction Catalog* to insure that the library is building a basic quality fiction collection." Or, a smaller library could state, "As a small public library, this library will purchase at least 80 percent of the fiction titles that *Booklist* lists as best of the year to insure the basic quality level of our adult, young adult, and juvenile collections."

Even though each library must set its own goals based on its budget and space availability, it's not difficult to insure that your collection includes appropriate "quality" fiction.

Popular reading materials

But—what about your patrons and what they *want* to read? When a library concentrates on purchasing "quality," that is not necessarily what its users want. How do we know what our patrons really want—and whether it's on the shelf when they want it? This kind of information can be quite valuable to a library, so one of the tools used in the Illinois project mentioned above was the Fiction Availability Survey shown at the right.

Using basic sampling theory guidelines, the libraries needed 125 valid responses to achieve a true sample of fiction availability in the library.

While it is preferable to conduct a survey such as this within one or two weeks, in some really small project libraries it took nearly a month to gather 125 responses, with several frequent patrons claiming they were being surveyed to death!

It might be helpful for other small libraries attempting such a survey to avoid patron anti-survey rebellion by doing what these libraries eventually did: staff would casually query patrons as they checked out their books to learn what they had been looking for, whether they found it or not, etc.—then the staff filled in the form for the patrons.

When the sample is tallied, the library will learn a good deal about how well it is meeting the fiction and genre reading needs of its patrons. None of the libraries

Individually small libraries collect at a minimal level (important authors, core titles); together, because of different acquisition criteria, they can be equal to a good, mid-sized collection with supplementary titles and multiple copies of key popular titles.

Fiction Availability Survey

1. What were you looking for today?

2. Did you find it?

3. Were you looking by title?

4. Were you looking by author?

5. Were you browsing by genre?

6. Which genre were you looking for?

participating in the Illinois project, even libraries in the smallest towns, had as good a handle on the fiction needs and wants of its patrons as staff thought they had. Using a Fiction Availability Survey gives a library input from its patrons that is very useful when making decisions about setting budgets for mysteries, science fiction, short stories, westerns, etc. Budget decisions will be based on data, not hunches.

Selection, retention, weeding

A selector of popular reading materials might follow some general purchasing guidelines:

> *When two people are waiting for a book, the library will order another copy.*
>
> *If five people are waiting for a title, we will purchase another copy from the local bookstore to get it into the collection as quickly as possible.*
>
> *If somebody comes in the front door and asks for a current book that we don't have, it will be ordered tomorrow.*

However, we need to extend that policy to the next logical step by stating:

> *If a popular title does not circulate at least once within a six-month period, then all but one copy will be withdrawn.*
>
> *If there have been no reserves for six months, and 75 percent of the copies are on the shelf, half are to be deaccessed.*

It might be easier to help justify these purchases and deaccessions, if, rather than thinking in terms of the amount of money spent on popular titles, we took into account how much they cost per use. After all, there can be an extraordinary amount of use in a short period of time. Compare the cost per use of popular titles to that of a well-reviewed quality title that has circulated twice in fifteen years.

Bear in mind that, if you weed popular titles fairly quickly after the demand tapers off, the books will still be high-demand book sale items—which gives the library another return on its investment in popular fiction.

We are all faced with weeding titles that no longer suit our collection parameters, but should still be available somewhere. This brings us to the next step, which is to take what you have learned about your collection and its use, and extend the information beyond your library collection to a local cooperative or across a regional system—particularly if the library is a member of a shared database. It could be fairly easy to develop retention plans based on what each of the libraries has learned about its collection and its use. Perhaps you would agree that you won't **discard** an Agatha Christie that does not circulate but is the only remaining copy in the database. Rather, you will **deaccess** Agatha to a partner library trying to build a complete collection of Christie's titles. Insuring retention of regional "last copies" is a win-win exercise in interlibrary cooperation—and an easy first venture into cooperative collection management for those still feeling tentative about the value of collection management partnerships.

Cooperative collection management

The role of cooperative collection management in fiction collections can go well beyond retention plans. Often libraries are involved in quasi or informal cooperatives, but find it hard to actually define, write down, and sign agreements that include any long-term and/or financial commitments.

When I first became involved with a formal cooperative collection management program, I remember thinking that I knew quite a bit about the field of cooperative collection management. After all, I had just come from a public library in a shared database where we "all" used the database to help formulate purchasing and retention decisions! We would search possible mystery purchases on the database. If we saw that Library X ordered a mystery title, we knew we had better buy it since our patrons seemed to have similar mystery "appetites". If there was a western that another library purchased, I didn't order it because by the time our western readers realized a new Louis L'Amour had been published, we could borrow it on interlibrary loan. It was so simple: no meetings, no written agreements, no commitments.

Well, I've since learned a bit more about the ins and outs of cooperative collection management. The scenario above could charitably be described as ad-hoc cooperative collection management. If you are to have true cooperative collection management, not only do you need to think a bit more carefully about what you are doing, your "partners" really should know that they are your partners! If Library X knew and accepted that they were being used as a benchmark for mysteries, they would let their partners know if changing finances or patron reading habits meant that they were revising their purchasing plans. If that other library knew that they were going to be my source for westerns, they would let me know about changes in their policies so that the reading needs of the five people who read westerns in my community could still be met.

No library has room for everything. More and more authors write multi-volume series or publish new titles at a phenomenal rate. It's no longer just young patrons who want to read every Nancy Drew or R. L. Stine; there are adults who want every Sue Grafton or title in a certain Harlequin series. I do the same thing— you probably do, too. We "discover" authors; we like them; we want to read everything they've written.

Libraries need to plan for this. A library should have room (on the shelves and in the budget) for a representative sample of fiction to meet the basic reading needs of their patrons, but few have the resources to meet the in-depth reading needs of each and every patron. This is why libraries should strongly consider developing cooperatives—so they can serve more than just basic patron needs. Partners in cooperatives are much like branches of a large library: each builds its own collection to best meet the needs of its community but relies on the other branches as sources for supplemental or additional titles.

Sampling and genre fiction

When studying fiction collections and their use, think a bit about what the library defines as fiction. There might be copies of *Great Expectations* in hardback, in paperback, on audio tape, or on video. All are fiction, but not all libraries consider them as part of the "fiction collection." Yet, depending on how the library is organized, one might wish to see whether classics or general fiction or mystery fiction are more popular with patrons who read large print or standard hardbacks or paperbacks. Are the library's patrons more likely to read the latest John Grisham or do they prefer listening to the audio tapes? How is fiction used in your library?

If a library would like to study or assess its fiction collection at the genre level or by format, but these are not cataloged or shelved separately, sampling techniques can be used to accomplish the task. As long as the sample includes at least

Before making any changes in how you manage your fiction collection, wouldn't it be a good idea to find out where your collection is now?

125 items, it is a true statistical sample. (Yes, it really is! I've done both sampling and item-by-item analyses. The results were essentially the same.) This means that it isn't necessary to look at the collection item by item to get a true picture of what you have in your fiction collections—and you can include all formats and media your library regards to be "fiction".

If the library has an automated bibliographic database, generate a printout of the database that lists every twenty-fifth book or whatever is needed to get to a sample of 125 fiction titles from the database. Then determine the genre and age of the title (and the circulation record, if you can). If the library maintains a card-file shelf list, measure the fiction shelf list, divide by 125, then measure an inch or half-inch or a quarter-inch of cards (or whatever is needed to get to 125 titles), pull out the card, and record the genre, age, and use data for the title. This is done for the entire fiction shelf list. If there is no shelf list, simply go to the shelves and the current circulation files and tally every twentieth item or circulation record (or whatever number is necessary to achieve a 125 item sample).

When you have completed your sample, you will have a clearer idea of what genres are in the collection—and by noting age and use of the materials, a library can see how the collection is developing or changing, genre by genre.

Conspectus / assessing the fiction collection

One fairly straightforward way of analyzing a complete fiction collection and its development is to use a conspectus or overview chart *(see fig. 1 on p.16)*. It's rather amazing how a conspectus can help you discover what you *really* have in your collection—and how the collection is developing compared to how you would like to see it develop!

Several library software vendors offer automated conspectus programs which enable a library to manipulate collection data in many ways. However, just to give you an idea of how a conspectus works, I've included a simple overview chart.

The big picture

This chapter has presented many different ways to look at, to think about, to study your fiction collection and its use. Rather than have bits and piece of information swirling about, you might wish to pull these strands together into a more coherent picture. If so, the Fiction Overview Chart I developed for Corn Belt Library System in Illinois (now part of the Alliance Library System) should help you do just that. It is a simple way to look at genre fiction in several different ways to form a composite view of each genre and of your fiction collection as a whole.

COLUMN 1: Holdings #/Level: Current holdings can be represented numerically (i.e.: 450 titles or 20 percent) or by using conspectus collection intensity indicators (i.e.: 1a).

COLUMN 2: Acquisition Level: Current annual additions also could be either numerical (20 titles; 2 percent) or by conspectus level (1b).

COLUMN 3: What number or percentage of your holdings in the genre is in non-book (audio, video) format?

COLUMN 4: When is the last time you weeded the collection?

COLUMN 5: Do you have a written collection policy for the area or is it mentioned specifically in your collection policy?

Fiction Overview

	Holdings #/ level	AQ Level	#Non Book	When weeded	Col Policy	CCM Area	CCM Respon	Heavy ILL	Heavy Ref	User Req
GENERAL FIC										
ADVENTURE										
CLASSICS										
FANTASY										
HISTORICAL										
HORROR										
MYSTERY										
ROMANCE										
SCI FI										
WESTERNS										
SHORT STORIES										
J FICTION										
J EASY FIC										
LARGE TYPE										
AUDIO										
VIDEO										

Fig. 1. Fiction Overview Chart developed for the Corn Belt Library System.

COLUMN 6: Are you involved in a cooperative collection management plan for this genre or format? Should you be thinking about a cooperative collection management plan for that genre or format?

COLUMN 7: If you are involved in a cooperative collection management plan, is there an area for which you have a purchasing or retention responsibility? This will make a difference in your overall purchasing and acquisition statistics. If your CCM responsibility is to insure that you have all the Stephen King books or a certain group of mystery authors, your chart (and budget) could appear skewed in areas where the library has a cooperative responsibility.

COLUMN 8: Is this an area of high interlibrary loan activity? Borrowing or lending?

COLUMN 9: Is this an area of heavy reference requests (for term papers or theses)?

COLUMN 10: Is this an area of heavy readers' advisory requests?

Completing this kind of overview chart will give you a quick, graphic representation of your fiction collection and its use. It can serve as a benchmark, a starting point from which to build a fiction collection that is more and more responsive to your user's needs. Redoing the chart on a regular basis (every three years or so) will help you verify that you are making progress—and identify changes in how the collection is being developed and used.

Using overview data

Use overviews and/or conspectus as a planning and developmental tool. Since conspectus subject and genre divisions are codified and because the collection intensity indicators have a uniform definition, the conspectus is an ideal tool to use when libraries work together to develop cooperative collection management plans. Since it is rare for a library to have too much money or too much space so that it doesn't have to rely on other libraries to help it meet patrons' needs, resource sharing is a fact of library life. The overview/conspectus is one way to bring science into that resource sharing.

> **The general recommendation is that you redo a conspectus or a formal study of your collection every three years**

It's not hard to see how this type of information could provide strong statistical support to requests for additional funds, for a need to weed, for an impetus to cooperative collection management. Naturally, the data must be collected and entered into a database (automated or manual)—and that involves the time librarians have in such short supply. Then, too, if you wish to be able to compare data over a range of years, the data must be gathered and entered again. It's not quite as bad as washing the dishes, but it is a bit like painting the living room. You have to redo it, but not every day. The general recommendation is that you redo a conspectus or a formal study of your collection every three years—pretty much like painting that living room.

If a library uses conspectus or overview data to justify making major changes in its collections and/or their development, it might want to revisit the study sooner than three years just to be sure the changes are working as planned. It's better to expend the effort on a re-study and catch mistakes early.

Cataloging fiction to serve readers

When *you* catalog fiction for *your* library, think about how *your* patrons look for fiction—and then do what you can to make it as easy as possible for them to find that they want.

1. Do you identify fiction by genre when cataloging?
2. Do you use genre stickers?
3. Do you shelve genres in separate, easily found sections?
4. Do you add fiction subject headings to the card catalog and/or the online catalog?
5. How many ways is your fiction collection searchable on the regional database?

It has been proven that the circulation of fiction increases when libraries shelve genres separately as bookstores do. In fact, the larger the library, the greater the increase in circulation. The bibliography at the end of the chapter lists titles by Shay (Sharon) Baker, who has done a great deal of research in the marketing of popular collections. Her research has led to some very strong arguments in favor of separating fiction by genre.

When Baker spoke about fiction collections at the 1988 Public Library Association Conference, she said that the key guideline is to catalog your books so they can be found by your patrons. How do people ask for books? Do people come in and ask for a title? More often than not, they will ask for an author, a type, or a subject. They'll ask for a setting (a Regency romance that takes place in London), the author's special slant on a genre (a techno-thriller), and they'll ask for these titles by accessibility (large print or English for new readers) and readability:

> "Can you help me find a good short novel that I can read on the beach next week?"

> "Please give me something nice and meaty that I can take up to the cottage. I'm going to be sitting there with a broken leg while everyone else is skiing."

When you think about how fiction is cataloged in your library, does this include paperbacks? Do you treat paperbacks with the respect they deserve?

1. How do you catalog them?

2. Are they added to the online catalog and/or the regional database?

3. How can they be searched on the database or in the card catalog?

4. Do you base decisions on use and demand or that somewhat elusive characteristic known as "quality"?

5. Are your decisions a type of censorship?

6. Should your inhouse cataloging of fiction and additions to the regional database take into consideration the kind of fiction you have the hardest time finding?

7. If so, then what is hardest type of fiction for you to find in your collection?

8. What is hardest for you to find on interlibrary loan?

Have you considered purchasing multiple copies of popular titles in *paperback*? Massachusetts' Salem Public Library presented a poster session at ALA in 1994 titled, *Stunned By the Obvious: Paperback Circulation and Multiple Buying—A Practical Application of the Quick Response Marketing Model*. The library conducted a seven-month experiment in increased multiple buying. For every hundred dollars spent on books, the library bought three times as many paperbacks as they bought hardbacks. They also bought more books to meet user demand at the time of demand—like a bookstore. In that seven-month time period, their circulation of paperbacks was 27,036; in a comparable seven month period in the previous year the circulation had been 11,415 —their paperback circulation increased 135 percent. Judging by the statistics, this is an approach that other libraries might well consider adopting!

It is also worth noting that libraries are discovering that paperbacks last just about as long as hardbacks, especially when the cover is reinforced with a laminate or even a clear contact paper. Even if the interior pages don't yellow, they are no less readable than the acid-based paper in older hardback books. Given the differences in the cost of a paperback and a hardback, shrinking budgets suggest that libraries should pay closer attention to the durability and popularity of paperback books. Then, too, libraries with space problems should consider paperbacks, simply because they take up less shelf space—both in height and in width.

As the former administrator of a multi-county interlibrary loan service in central Illinois, I can assure you that our staff was more often thwarted attempting to track down a fairly recent Harlequin romance than when looking for an early Erle Stanley Gardner mystery!

Cataloging like a bookstore

Just like a bookstore, libraries want patrons to come in, look around, and take some of our product home with them. But, beyond an inviting ambiance, author signings, and special promotions, what else does a bookstore do to entice customers to stay, to browse, to spend?

Think about what *you* do when you go to a bookstore. How do you find what you want? Is it easier for you to find what you want in a bookstore or your library? (Actually, you probably are too familiar with your own library, so it would be better to test that question by going to another library!) Powell's Book Store in Portland, Oregon, sells both new and used books. Books are separated by genre or subject and then interfiled by author so both the new books and the used books are together much as in a library. This is wonderful for most customers who know the general areas and genres in which they are interested. However, Powell's goes one step further; they have large sections devoted to new books, where *additional* copies of these titles are displayed.

Most bookstores don't seem to have a problem with shelving copies of a book in more than one place. If a book has strong elements of historical fiction and fantasy, copies will be displayed in both sections. If it's a steamy fantasy fiction, copies will be found in the romance section as well as in fantasy/science fiction. Naturally, the bookstore is looking for sales, so they feel it is in their best interest to insure that the right book is in the right place for the *customer* to find it—not in the one place in the store that fits an arcane set of rules set by the inventory control staff. Well, essentially, aren't libraries trying to get users to "buy" their product—books? It was the first Marshall Field who said, "Give the lady what she wants"—and he was rather successful. Beyond budgetary constraints, are there any truly valid reasons for libraries to insist that cataloged titles are to be in only one place in the library? If we can have video and audio versions of *Little Women* in different places in the library, can't we have hardbacks in both the children's and adult collections—and perhaps paperback copies in both children's and young adult areas—and another copy with displays of popular novels by nineteenth century women authors and of books made into films?

What about that relatively new concept in manufacturing called "just in time"? What about a "just in time" fiction collection? Wouldn't you like to be a step ahead when a patron presents you with a slightly garbled title mentioned on *Oprah* "a few days ago"? The bi-weekly *Get Ready Sheet* from Mid York Library System lists authors and their titles and the talk shows on which they will be appearing, as well as the book versions of upcoming TV shows and movies. This, along with the Yellow Pages in the Baker & Taylor *Forecast*, the Upfront and Pre Pub Alert sections in *Booklist* and *Library Journal*, enables you to be a little bit ahead of your patrons, even if you can't afford to subscribe to *Publisher's Weekly* and *Kirkus*.

Final thoughts

Only you can answer this question: Are you giving your fiction collection the respect it deserves?

Readers are different in different genres; readers are different in different communities. Librarians should become comfortable with the concept that the collection is being developed for the users, not for convenience of the cataloging department or the shelvers or your favorite library school professor. You are bound by budget constraints and the physical layout of your building, but you can still make the likes and wants of your readers the driving force behind the development of your fiction collection as much as you can.

There are as many ways of handling fiction as there are libraries—and the

Circulation time periods

Sarah Parker, former State Librarian of Pennsylvania and now of Missouri, has been quoted as saying, "Libraries have to stop doing the things that make us look stupid." Well, when a library takes a "hot" new book that everybody wants to read and puts it on a seven-day loan period so that more people have a chance to read it, it seems like a good idea—until you come up with that hot new book that happens to be 1400 pages long. That's almost like seduction and betrayal; seduce the patron into beginning the relationship and then betray them by withdrawing the object of affection before the relationship is consummated!

only right one is the one that works in *your* library for *your* community. And if it doesn't work the first or second time, see what other libraries are doing, look at the local bookstore, and "play around" with different ideas. There is no reason why a public library that thinks about what it is doing, ought not to have a good fiction collection that is increasingly well used by its community.

Managing fiction collections: Some resources

Baker, Sharon L., Project Consultant, *Fiction Collection Assessment Manual*. Champaign, Illinois: Lincoln Trail Libraries System, 1992.

———and F. Wilfred Lancaster, *The Measurement and Evaluation of Library Services*. 2nd ed., Information Resources Press, 1991.

———, *The Responsive Public Library Collection: How to Develop and Market It*. Englewood, CO: Libraries Unlimited, 1993.

Guide for Written Collection Policy Statements. Chicago: American Library Association, 1989.

Hennepin County Library Materials Selection Section Collection and Special Services Section, *Hennepin County Library Collection Maintenance Manual*. Minnetonka, Minnesota: Hennepin County Library System, revised 1988.

Olson, Georgine N. and Barbara McFadden Allen, eds., "Fiction Assessment," pp. 63–86, *Cooperative Collection Management: The Conspectus Approach*. New York: Neal-Schuman, 1994. Also published as special issue of *Collection Building*, v.13 #2-3.

WLN Conspectus Software. Lacey, Washington: WLN, January 1995.

Do You Have Any Good Books Here?
Readers' Advisory Work for Children

Chapter Three   Susan Strunk and Mary Ellen Middleton

The inspiration for this chapter came from a child who approached a librarian at our information desk one day. He asked, "Do you have any good books here?" Of course she knew there were many good books and even many great books in the library; and after a short conversation with the boy, she was able to help him choose a few books that seemed to meet his requirements for a "good" book. His question, however, has stayed with the library staff. Seeing hundreds of items on the shelves, he still wasn't confident that the library really had anything that he might want to read. This is the whole point of offering readers' advisory service to children—to help them connect with the materials they want or need. But as many librarians have found, the tricky thing about working with children is that they often don't know what they like to read, and if they do know, it may still be very difficult for them to explain it to someone else. It is even more difficult for them to label their reading preferences with the name of a particular category such as mystery, science fiction, or fantasy.

To get past these barriers, the professional literature concerning readers' advisory service recommends establishing a relationship with readers so that we can better understand their reading interests and needs. This certainly is the ideal. All of us who have been lucky enough to spend sufficient time with a patron over a period of repeat visits to develop a relationship will agree this is the best way to help him choose what he will truly find most enjoyable. But realistically, we don't usually have this opportunity. Often we don't even recognize the child who asks for reading guidance and even less often do we know his name. Frequently it is parents who are asking us to recommend a book, especially if the book is to be read for a school assignment or if they feel that their child is a "reluctant" reader. The child for whom we are to make a recommendation may not even be present! Still, whether we know the child well or not, whether the book is to be read as a school assignment or just for fun and whether the child is absent or present, when the request for help is made, we do whatever we can in hopes the reader will experience pleasure in reading the recommended title.

To experience pleasurable reading, according to Victor Nell, author of *Lost in a Book: The Psychology of Reading for Pleasure*, three factors must be present. They are 1) a high degree of reading competency, 2) positive expectations about reading, and 3) correct book selection. Nell calls this reading for pleasure "ludic" reading from the Latin word *ludo* which means "to play." Ultimately it will be the child who decides whether or not the book we help select is a "good" book, but Nell gives us some guidelines by suggesting three qualities of a good book. They are:

1. literary merit,

2. difficulty (vocabulary and sentence length), and

3. trance potential (defined as the perceived capacity of a book to exercise dominion and superiority). *A reader's perceived "trance potential" can often override merit or difficulty.*

What we are trying to determine when we conduct a readers' advisory interview is not only what the child has enjoyed, but also why he has enjoyed it. There most certainly is a connection between how a book makes a reader feel and how much he enjoys the book. Especially as children approach and enter adolescence, they will be led to reading interests through their emotions rather than through intellect. They want "trance potential"!

In this chapter, our aim is to share some tools we have found useful in making us more effective readers' advisors. We continue to use these tools with the intent of always sending the reader home with at least one "good" book.

Creating a children's genre list

The purpose of this activity is to get you to think of some broad categories of children's fiction and then to group authors under the categories. This list is the foundation for conducting an organized study of children's fiction. The list we are creating is based on the concept of the "popular fiction list" as described in *Readers' Advisory Service in the Public Library* by Saricks and Brown.

We encourage you to use the outline form on the next page to start your children's genre list; adding or changing categories to match your collection will make the list more effective. Fill in authors from your own collections—here, we have provided just one name in each section and a starter list of prominent authors in the field of children's literature. Of course, a list of authors and the type of books they write will be of little value to you if you do not have any books by these authors in your collections! Use your own knowledge of what authors write or look at resources like *Best Books for Children* or *The Children's Catalog* to identify the most prolific authors in the different categories.

Having created your list of genres and authors, how might you use the list in your library? First, it could serve as a reading list for you and any other staff who serve children. Each staff member could read an author from a particular genre. Sharing the plots, themes and styles of these books would thoroughly acquaint everyone with the range of authors in that genre. Another approach would be to assign a genre to one person who then becomes the genre "expert" and shares with the rest of the staff. When new employees arrive in the department, the list will help them become familiar with major children's authors quickly and will give them a starting point to begin reading juvenile fiction.

The list certainly does not have to remain fixed and as new authors appear on the scene or as established authors begin to write in other genres, you can update your list to maintain a current representation of major authors in the different categories.

As you read through the different authors within the genres, recordkeeping will be important so that you and others on your staff can remember important

Children's Genre List

Mystery	Science Fiction
1. Roberts, Willo Davis	1. Sleator, William
2.	2.
3.	3.
4.	4.
5.	5.
6.	6.
7.	7.
8.	8.
9.	9.
10.	10.

Realistic Fiction	Humorous
1. Blume, Judy	1. Sachar, Louis
2.	2.
3.	3.
4.	4.
5.	5.
6.	6.
7.	7.
8.	8.
9.	9.
10.	10.

Historical Fiction	High Fantasy
1. Collier, James	1. Christopher, John
2.	2.
3.	3.
4.	4.
5.	5.
6.	6.
7.	7.
8.	8.
9.	9.
10.	10.

Magical Fantasy	Supernatural
1. Eager, Edward	1. Wright, Betty Ren
2.	2.
3.	3.
4.	4.
5.	5.
6.	6.
7.	7.
8.	8.
9.	9.
10.	10.

Adams, Douglas
Adler, C.S.
Alexander, Lloyd
Asimov, Isaac
Avi
Babbitt, Natalie
Beatty, Patricia
Bellairs, John
Blume, Judy
Bond, Michael
Brittain, Bill
Bunting, Eve
Byars, Betsy
Chetwin, Grace
Christian, Mary Blount
Clifford, Eth
Collier, James
Cooper, Susan
Cross, Gillian
Dahl, Roald
Delton, Judy
Duncan, Lois
Eager, Edward
Fleischman, Sid
George, Jean Craighead
Giff, Patricia Reilly
Greene, Constance
Greenwald, Sheila
Hahn, Mary Downing
Hoover, H.M.
Howe, James
Jurwitz, Johanna
Jacques, Brian
Key, Alexander
King-Smith, Dick
Kjelgaard, James
Kline, Suzy
Lawlor, Laurie
L'Engle, Madeline
Lewis, C.S.
MacLachlan, Patricia
McGowen, Tom
McKinley, Robin
Milne, A.A.
Naylor, Phyllis Reynolds
Norton, Andre
O'Dell, Scott
Paulsen, Gary
Pinkwater, Daniel
Raskin, Ellen
Rinaldi, Ann
Rylant, Cynthia
Sleator, William
Sobol, Donald
Tolkein, J.R.R.
Voight, Cynthia
White, E.B.
Wilder, Laura I.
Yolen, Jane

Fig. 3.1. Children's Genre List format sample.

information about each book. The idea is to get the facts about a book, book-on-tape or video down on paper, before you forget the plot. Or, if you do remember the plot, you may find to your great irritation that you can't remember the title that goes with that plot. File the cards by genre and you will have a source to go to for periodic memory refreshment or to use on those days when your mind goes absolutely blank in the middle of a readers' advisory interaction.

Genre _____

Circle one: J   YA   (reading level _____   interest level _____)

Title _____

Author _____

Pub year _____   Number of pages _____

Summary and commentary _____

_____

_____

_____

_____

_____

_____

Similar authors or books: _____

Reader's name _____   Date: _____

Fig. 3.2. Genre Reading Report Forms: Any similar record-keeping device will be effective.

Booktalk: A discussion group for children

Mary Ellen Middleton

Some children, like some adults, derive great pleasure from talking with others about the books they have read. Booktalk is a book discussion group offered for 4th and 5th graders at the Naperville Libraries.

Children have much to gain by participating in a book discussion group. Their understanding of genres, authors, titles, and some of the elements of writing increases. They broaden their reading experience by reading books that they might not normally pick out for themselves and thus discover new books to read. It is very important to me, as the discussion leader, to maintain a nonthreatening and nonjudgmental atmosphere. Those children who feel intimidated by large discussion groups such as those found in classrooms, feel more comfortable discussing in a small group.

Book discussions with children have a very positive impact on the discussion leader. I find it is a golden opportunity to establish a relationship with some of the children who come into our busy library. My awareness of children's reading preferences is effectively raised. Like the kids, I read books that I wouldn't normally choose and learn about new titles to read.

Structuring a program

Because of the need for participants to read one book per week in preparation for the discussions, it truly is for those children who are there of their own free will and not because a parent says they must. I can quickly pick out the unhappy ones. The maximum number that I have allowed to register is twelve. With more than that, not all the kids get a chance to participate. We have had a series of six and eight discussions. I prefer eight as it gives us more opportunity to solidify as a group.

Our meetings have been held after school once a week from 4:00 to 5:00. Because there are a variety of ways to organize book discussions, I like to vary the organization within a series of discussions to make it more interesting and to broaden the appeal.

The most commonly used format is that in which all participants read the same book. Some criteria for choosing a single book are:

1. There must be enough copies of the book available.
2. It must not have so many pages that kids would not be able to finish it in a week. (Keep the choice under 150 pages.)
3. It must be age-appropriate and appeal to girls and boys alike.
4. It must have the potential for discussion.
5. It must have kid appeal and some literary merit.

(Some of the titles that we have used for discussion are: *The Whipping Boy, Abel's Island, The Cay* and *Beauty.*)

Discussion of a single author in which participants choose any book by the author is another format. Obviously, the author must have written multiple titles which have appeal for both boys and girls. (Authors we have used are Avi, Roald Dahl, and Gary Paulsen.)

In a genre discussion, participants choose a book from a designated genre such as supernatural, mystery, science fiction, adventure or humor.

Leading the discussion

Although I know that the kids have discussed books in school, the first meeting is always an introductory session. I begin with personal introductions asking the kids their grade, school, and the title of their current favorite book.

Next, I share a few guidelines for our meetings. I tell them that I make two assumptions about those who register for Booktalk. One is that they like to read for pleasure and the other is that they like to talk about what they've read. I tell them that I know there are many demands on their time, but they should do their very best to have their book read for the next week so they will be able to contribute more to the discussion.

Also, there are no right or wrong answers to the questions, there are only opinions. I often ask the children to backup their opinions with evidence from the book. The children are encouraged to agree or disagree with comments made by other group members. To make the discussion more lively, I try to get them to not raise their hands when they want to speak—but this is a hard habit to break. Also, no one may interrupt another.

To give the participants an idea of what the discussions will be like, I might show a portion of a filmstrip such as *The Great Gilly Hopkins* or *Dear Mr. Henshaw* and then pose a few questions for a brief discussion. When they leave, they take the next week's book with them.

The subsequent meetings begin with a literature-based games such as "Hangman" with the titles of books. When the group reads from the fantasy genre, I have

A sample Booktalk program might consist of the following discussions:

Week 1. Introduction

Week 2. Discussion of the *The Dollhouse Murders* by Betty Ren Wright

Week 3. Discussion of work by Avi

Week 4. Discussion of poetry

Week 5. Discussion of *Shades of Gray* by Carol Reeder

Week 6. Discussion of the supernatural genre

Week 7. Discussion of work by Gary Paulsen

Week 8. Discussion of *Real Dog* by Bill Wallace

the kids take two minutes to choose any three books from juvenile fiction. We then go around the group three times creating a fantasy story in which each one's addition to the story must include the title of one of the books they chose. When we have all read the same book, the leader prepares questions for a "Battle of the Book" played in two teams. This is always a hit. There are times that I question the value of the games and wonder if our time would be better spent just on the book discussion. However, the kids really enjoy the games and since one of the goals is for the kids to have a positive library experience, I think they are worth continuing.

When our discussion is the work of one author, I always include a brief biographical sketch. I try to include details of the author's life that would be of particular interest to the kids and that are particularly related to the books read. For example, if we have all read different books by Gary Paulsen, I might point out that like Brian in *Hatchet*, Paulsen has survived the wilderness with little to sustain him. The biographical information comes from sources such as *Something About the Author, Contemporary Authors, Book Links,* and *Publishers Weekly.*

Before I even get a chance to ask the first question, the kids are always ready with a personal response to the book. I often ask them to rate the book like movies are rated. "How many stars would you give the book, with four being the highest?" They are tough critics!

If we have read from a specific genre, I spend a few minutes talking about the characteristics of the genre. For example, I might ask what they would expect to find in a supernatural story or a survival story. This identification helps them to learn to distinguish between genres.

When we have all read different books, rather than asking them to just tell us what their book was about, I might ask, "Tell us who the main character is and something about his or her personality" or "What was the mystery that was being solved?" or in the case of the adventure genre, "What was the setting and what kind of a role did it play in the adventure?"

With each discussion, I try to spend just a short time highlighting a particular element of writing. "What descriptive words or what incidents in the story gave you a sense of where the story took place?" In talking about character, I ask if a character is someone they would like to have for a friend, and then, why or why not. Or "Did the main character seem like a real person?" In addressing a theme, I might ask, "Why did the author write this story? Did she or he have something to say to the reader?"

Because I have been trained as a Great Books discussion leader and have led Great Books discussions for grades 3 through 8, I also ask interpretive questions taking the kids to a deeper level of thinking. Examples might be, "Was it a blessing or a curse that the Tucks drank the water?" or "On page 103, before Abel is about to leave the island, the author tells us that he looks back at it with 'sudden anguish.' How did Abel feel about leaving the island?" I often conclude the discussion by asking each one if they feel any differently about the book after discussion.

The session ends with either a distribution of the book for the next meeting or, in the case of the author and genre discussions, the children choosing a book from the selection that I have pulled. If there is time, I briefly tell them something about some of the titles.

I feel that the key to a successful discussion is thorough preparation on my part. I always read the book at least two times and come prepared with questions in order to keep the discussion moving along smoothly.

If you have the time and resources, I encourage you to seriously consider offering book discussion groups for your young patrons. This has been a very effective way to stay in tune with what our young readers like to read, which results in more effective readers' advisory service.

Personal reading advisors

In my experience as a children's librarian, it is not often that a child will ask, "Can you recommend a good mystery with a supernatural element?" or "I really like a book with a strong female heroine. Do you have any to recommend?" I have speculated that the reasons may be that the reader is unaware of the types of books he or she likes to read because they do not understand the concept of genres or the child is too shy to talk to an unfamiliar adult. Young patrons may also not realize that helping them find recreational reading is as much a part of my job as helping them find the annual rainfall in Havana.

The Personal Reading Advisor program was conceived during the holiday season a few years ago when I saw that department stores were offering personal shopping services for the "too-busy" or the "shopping challenged." At about the same time I had once again been noticing young patrons wandering the fiction stacks looking for just the right book and being challenged by the number of books from which to choose. When I approached them with the offer of assistance, they often would reply that they did not need any help, but they continued to look. And maybe they didn't need help. Some were probably perfectly happy to browse and discover new books to read for themselves. But there are some young readers who I felt certain would have welcomed some recommendations.

For those who would like book recommendations, but hesitate to ask, the Personal Reading Advisor program offers the opportunity to specify reading preferences by completing a written questionnaire. The questionnaire is designed to identify reading preferences by using some of the same questions asked in a readers' advisory interview.

The questionnaire (*see figure 3 on p. 34*) first asks for the identity of the reader including name, address, phone number, gender, age, grade, and school. Then many genres are listed and the readers are asked to circle those that they like to read. The next two questions pertain to books read recently that were liked and those not liked in order to ascertain not only the type of book preferred, but also the reading level. It is always interesting to read the answer to the next question which asks what is the best book he or she has ever read. The respondent is then asked who is their favorite author. To get a sense of whether we are dealing with a voracious or reluctant reader, we ask them to indicate if they read whenever they can, occasionally or never. The next question asks if there is anything else that they can tell us about what they like to read. The last two questions which query general interests ask what their favorite animal is and what their hobbies or extracurricular activities are.

At our libraries the questionnaires are displayed and readily available at the Information Desks. To a completed questionnaire we attach a suggestion sheet and then circulate it among those staff members who read from Juvenile and Young Adult fiction. Once this is completed, another staff member writes the suggested titles on a final book list that is then given to the reader. The process takes about one to two weeks from the time the questionnaire is turned in until the child is called to pick up his or her completed reading list.

After using the program for a year at the Batavia Public Library and for the last two years at the Naperville Libraries, the heaviest use has been among girls ages

Besides our own personal reading, some of the sources we have used for finding titles to recommend are:

Gillespie and Naden. *Best Books for Children: Preschool Through Grade 6.*

Gillespie. *Best Books for Junior High Readers.*

New York Public Library. *Books for the Teen Age.*

Trelease, Jim. *The New Read-Aloud Handbook*

Personal Reading List Questionnaire
For independent readers of "J" or "YA" fiction

Dear Reader,

With all the books that are in the library, we know that it is often difficult to choose a book to read. You can ask a friend, brother, or sister for suggestions, but what they enjoy reading, may not be what you enjoy. Everyone has different tastes in reading. So we have designed this program to help.

By answering completely all the questions below, you will provide us with the information we need to create a reading list of ten books just for you!

Name _____

Address _____

Phone Number _____

Age _____ Grade_____ School _____

Circle: Boy Girl

Circle where you will pick up your list: Nichols Library Naper Blvd. Library

1. Circle the types of books you like to read:

Historical fiction	Time travel	Sports	Adventure	Scary
Science fiction	Supernatural	Mystery	Humor	Fantasy
Family stories	Animal stories	School stories	Biographies	Poetry

Nonfiction (What subject area?) _____

Other type of book not mentioned_____

2. What book or books did you read **most recently** *that you liked?*_____
_____

3. What book or books did you read **most recently** *that you did not like?* _____
_____

4. What are some of the **best** books you have ever read? _____
_____

5. If you have a favorite author, who is it? If there is more than one, we'd like to know. _____
_____

6. Put a check mark by the sentence that best describes your reading habits.

_____ I read whenever I can. Reading is what I do for pleasure.

_____ I read occasionally. There are some other things I'd rather do for pleasure.

_____ I never read for pleasure. I'd rather do almost anything else.

7. Is there anything else you can tell us about what you like to read? _____

8. Do you have a favorite animal? _____ What? _____

9. What are your hobbies or activities outside of school? _____
_____

Fig. 3. Personal Reading List Questionnaire from the Naperville Public Libraries, Youth Services Department.

nine, ten, and eleven. They love it! In fact, we now have two girls for whom we have completed three book lists. We have also had very positive comments from parents and teachers who find the program very beneficial particularly for their reluctant readers. If we have had a conversation with a parent about the reading habits of a child and know that information is relevant to the suggestions, we note it on the questionnaire.

I feel strongly that this program has been as beneficial for the staff as it has for the readers. I know it has greatly improved my readers' advisory skills. It has reinforced for me how much kids love scary, mysterious, humorous books. Based on a tally of the genre preferences indicated on the 60 questionnaires completed in the last year, if you are thinking of writing a juvenile book, a humorous mystery/ adventure about a family of animals would be a bestseller!

Bibliographies: Creating links

We often feel that the biggest challenge in readers' advisory service is working with a child who is just about ready to make a transition from one level or type of reading to a another. Creating the link from one part of the collection to another is a major service we can provide to both children and parents. Creating links among books or types of books is also a way to help children diversify what they are reading. We have found bibliographies to be an extremely useful way to create these links in a very unobtrusive manner. Let's look at some of the lists we use in our library.

We keep these lists out on the shelves. "After Board Books" is with the board books. "Very First Chapter Books" is kept above the beginning readers. The list of books similar to *Goosebumps* is displayed right near the *Goosebumps* books or at least near where the *Goosebumps* books should be if any are in! The list of transitional chapter books is within an arm's reach of the juvenile fiction. We want the lists to be available right where the patron is going to need them. We try to anticipate the need of the readers and answer some questions before they are asked. You may have some different needs for your library and so can create your own links with bibliographies.

Displays, AV and miscellaneous ideas

Displays can be one way to entice readers to choose a "good" book. Virtually every library I have been in has had one sort of book or material display. They are appealing, eye-catching, and usually effective. Books in a display seem to disappear almost as fast as you can add them to the display. Readers tend to be very trusting when it comes to displays. They believe that we are "in the know" and will most certainly only put the very best items out on display. So, we do have some responsibility to choose carefully what we display. Dorothy Broderick (see bibliography) has even gone so far as to say that every display we set up or booklist we create is a statement of our value system. Why display one item but not another is a question she feels we should ask ourselves.

Another display that we've had up for quite a while is our "Author of the Month" and "Illustrator of the Month" feature. Every month or so we post a picture and biographical information about one children's author and one illustrator of children's books. We load the display with samples of their work. We believe this is a simple way to introduce children and parents to good literature and dynamite artwork.

One more note about having an unobtrusive impact on children's reading is that if we believe certain titles from among picture books or chapter books offer

Very First Chapter Books

Beginning readers, who are looking for books with very short chapters, might enjoy books by the following authors. These easy chapter books can be found on the shelves labeled Readers. (Books by Howe and Delton can be found in J Fiction)

Baker, Barbara
Byars, Betsy
Coerr, Eleanor
Delton, Judy *(in J Fiction)*
Howe, James *(in J Fiction)*
Impey, Rose
Krensky, Stephen
Lobel, Arnold
Luttrell, Ida
Marshall, James
Pilkey, Dave
Prager, Annabelle
Ross, Pat

Give thought to how you label displays.

We set up a display called "May We Recommend?" It was a display on which we placed books either we ourselves had enjoyed or which had been well reviewed. We divided It into two sections—books for 3rd and 4th graders and books for 5th and 6th graders. Very quickly after setting up the display we noticed that children would only look at books for their own grade level and were ignoring books which they might have very well enjoyed but which were in the other half of the display. So we took down the grade labels and simply put out books with a wide range of interests and reading levels. We liked this better because it gave the readers many more choices from among many good books!

something special to a child or should be a part of children's general literacy, then we owe it to them to have sufficient copies available so that the title is on the shelf more often than not! When children or parents see multiple copies of an item on the shelf, it is reasonable to assume that they will think, "Oh, that must be a really good book; look how many copies they have!"

Be alert to the fact that sometimes a book alone may not be necessarily the best recommendation for a child. I have at times persuaded a reader to try the book-on-tape of certain titles and quite honestly have had mixed reviews. Some have enjoyed listening. Others admitted that they later came in and checked out the book, but did enjoy listening to the book-on-tape while they were reading the book. A few simply preferred reading to listening. I will sometimes recommend that the patron check out both the book and the book-on-tape when the reading is for a school assignment. I do this especially if the child and/or parent is expressing concern about the length of the book or the perceived difficulty level. We do need to be aware of the value of audiovisual materials as part of our readers' advisory program.

Electronic sources of information offer a growing set of resources that can enhance our readers' advisory capabilities. Databases and indexes on CD-ROM and listservs on the Internet are examples of resources that are becoming increasingly available. Perhaps with this technology, we will be able to conduct searches on book features such as number of pages, level of reading difficulty, book character types and plot situations. Of course, as we all know, "number of pages" is the single most important attribute of any book a child has to read for a school assignment.

In closing, I quote again Victor Nell, who so clearly supports our reason for believing so strongly in the value of quality readers' advisory service to children. "The public does not value the library's collection because of its size or its breadth or its depth. A library's collection is valued for the stories it contains."

Miscellaneous thoughts about readers' advisory

"I don't like that book" is reason enough and it admits no arguments. *(Barbara Rollock)*

"People," a word that includes children, have a right to like books without our approval. *(Dorothy Broderick)*

"There's a tendency for librarians to find children who like to read what the librarian likes to read and then call it readers' advisory." *(Mae Benne)*

Children's read-alike bibliography

Compiled by Evelyn Vanek

Goosebumps - "Do you have any books like the Goosebumps books?"

Avi. *Something Upstairs*. New York: Orchard Books, 1988.

> Kenny feels that there is something upstairs in his new house. He's right!

Bellairs, John. *Vengeance of the Witch-Finder*. New York: Dial Books for Young Readers, 1993.

> The third book in The House with a Clock in Its Walls series. Lewis and his uncle travel to Europe, and accidently unleash the ghost of Malachiah Pruitt.

Cohen, Daniel. *Great Ghosts*. New York: Cobblehill, 1990.

> Decide for yourself. Are these ghosts real?

Hahn, Mary Downing. *Wait Till Helen Comes*. New York: Clarion, 1986.

> Molly and Michael are forced to put up with Heather, but end up trying to save her from the mysterious Helen.

Hildick, E. W. *Ghost Squad and the Menace of the Malevs*. New York: Dutton, 1988.

> The Ghost Squad must stop a killer—and a powerful superghost.

Jacques, Brian. *Seven Strange and Ghostly Tales*. New York: Philomel, 1991.

> Seven original ghost stories by the author of the Redwall series.

Naylor, Phyllis Reynolds. *Witch's Eye.* New York: Delacorte, 1990.

   The witch is dead, but her magic eye is not!

Peck, Richard. *The Ghost Belonged to Me.* New York: Viking, 1975.

   A hilarious story involving psychics, ghosts, and adventures along the Mississippi during the early 1900s.

Sleator, William. *Among the Dolls.* New York: Dutton, 1975.

   Vicky wanted a bike, not a dollhouse—especially not a musty, antique dollhouse. Gradually she gets used to it, but then, something shocking happens!

———. *Into the Dream.* New York: Dutton, 1979.

   Paul has the same dream over and over, and it becomes more and more intense. Francine has the dream, too. They are both drawn to Noah, a small child, and make an amazing discovery.

Sommer-Bodenburg, Angela. *If You Want to Scare Yourself.* New York: Lippencott, 1989.

   Freddy is hurt and must stay in bed, but he is entertained by his family members as they tell him scary stories. Then he makes up his own! (gr. 3-4)

Walsh, Jill Paton. *Birdy and the Ghosties.* New York: Farrar Straus Giroux, 1989.

   A mysterious old woman helps birdy discover her special powers. (gr. 3-4)

Wright, Betty Ren. *Ghost of Popcorn Hill.* New York: Holiday House, 1993.

   In trying to rid their room of a ghost. Peter and Martin discover that this isn't the only ghost around. (gr. 3-4)

Babysitters Club –"What can I read that's like the Babysitters Club?"

Conford, Ellen. *Anything for a Friend.* Boston: Little Brown, 1979.

   Wallis moves a lot, and once again is faced with fitting in and making friends.

———. *Me and the Terrible Two.* Boston: Little Brown, 1974.

   In this delightful story, Dorrie must deal with new neighbors who are twins, and in the process learns a lesson in friendship.

Hermes, Patricia. *Kevin Corbett Eats Flies.* San Diego: Harcourt Brace Jovanovich, 1986.

   Bailey and Kevin, originally rivals, find themselves allies in a battle of wits against the "grown ups."

Herzig, Allison. *Ten-Speed Babysitter.* New York: Dutton, 1987.

   Babysitting a toddler sounds like easy money for Tony, but he's in for a big surprise.

Hurwitz, Johanna. *Tough-luck Karen.* New York: William Morrow, 1982.

   Karen is failing all her subjects, and discovers that she has to make her own luck.

Kassem, Lou. *Middle School Blues.* Oakland, CA: Parnassus Press, 1986.

   Cindy finds middle school a challenge and, finding no help in books on adolescence, decides to write her own "10 Rules for Survival."

Lord, Bette. *In the Year of the Boar and Jackie Robinson.* New York: Harper & Row, 1984.

   Shirley Temple Wong, newly arrived from China, is fascinated with America, but she has no friends. Baseball changes all that.

Lowry, Lois. *Anastasia Krupnik.* Boston: Houghton Mifflin, 1979.

   Anastasia is delightful, precocious, and has unlimited self-confidence. This is the first book of many that follow her adventures.

————. *Taking Care of Terrific.* Boston: Houghton Mifflin, 1983.

> Follow the babysitting adventures of 14-year-old Enid as she copes with the life and 4-year-old Joshua, alias Tom Terrific.

Martin, Ann. *Stage Fright.* New York: Holiday House, 1984.

> Sara has to deal with being shy, stage fright, and her best friend moving away. She finds she's stronger that she thinks.

McMullan, Kate. *Great Ideas of Lila Fenwick.* New York: Dial Books for Young Readers, 1986.

> Lila has an ingenious solution to every problem, with hilarious results.

Naylor, Phyllis Reynolds. *The Agony of Alice.* New York: Atheneum, 1985.

> Alice is about to become a teenager, and has no idea how to be a teenaged girl. Her search for a role model results in some amazing discoveries.

Perl, Lila. *Tybee Trimble's Hard Times.* New York: Clarion, 1984.

> Tybee's family is having financial difficulties, so she decides to earn her own money to go to the circus for a school project.

Robinson, Nancy. *Just Plain Cat.* New York: Four Winds Press, 1981.

> Chris has gotten off to a bad start in third grade. Perhaps a cat will help.

Sachs, Marilyn. *The Bear's House.* Garden City, NY: Doubleday, 1971.

> Fran Ellen uses humor and determination to deal with some very difficult situations.

Sharmat, Marjorie. *Getting Something on Maggie Marmelstein.* New York: Harper & Row, 1971.

> Thad and Marjorie wage a perpetual war of one-upsmanship. How will their "contest" end?

Shura, Mary Francis. *Polly Panic.* New York: Putnam, 1990.

> Polly faces sixth grade and some difficult decisions, and gains new confidence in herself.

Van Leeuwen, Jean. *Dear Mom, You're Ruining My Life.* New York: Dial Books for Young Readers, 1989.

> Samantha has turned eleven, and she is worried about everything.

Wallace, Bill. *Ferret in the Bedroom, Lizards in the Fridge.* New York: Holiday House, 1986.

> Liz has decided that her father's collection of unusual animals is ruining her chances at winning the class election.

Children's readers' advisory: Some resources

Note: For general reference sources on genre fiction see Selected Professional References beginning on p. 109.

Benne, Mae. *Principles of Children's Services in Public Libraries.* Chicago: American Library Association, 1991.

Broderick, Dorothy M. *Library Work with Children.* New York: H.W. Wilson, 1977.

Broderick, Dorothy M. "How to Write a Fiction Annotation." *Voice of Youth Advocates: VOYA* (February 1993): 333.

Chelton, Mary K. "Read Any Good Books Lately?" *Library Journal* 118, no.8 (1 May 1993): 33/37.

Edwards, Margaret. *The Fair Garden and the Swarm of Beasts: The Library and the Young Adult.* New York: Hawthorn Books, 1974.

Langer, Lois, Wendy Woodfill, and Mary Weber. "Children's Book Discussion Groups." *Public Libraries* 32, no.6 (November/December 1993): 315-17.

McCook, Kathleen De La Pena, ed. *Developing Readers' Advisory Services: Concepts and Commitments.* New York: Neal-Schuman, 1993.

Nell, Victor. *Lost in a Book: The Psychology of Reading for Pleasure.* New Haven, CT: Yale University Press, 1988.

Rollock, Barbara. *Public Library Services for Children.* Hamden, CT: Library Professional Publications, 1988.

Sampley, Lisa. "Readers' Advisory Notes." *The Unabashed Librarian.* no. 80 (November 1991): 24.

Saricks, Joyce G. and Nancy Brown. *Readers' Advisory Service in the Public Library.* Chicago: American Library Association, 1989.

Sharp, Peggy A. "I Need a Good Book...Fast: A 60 Second Strategy for Selecting a Book to Read." *School Library Media Activities Monthly* 8 (April 1992): 30-31.

Connecting Readers' Advisors

Chapter Four

Tired of the same old workshops on databases to improve your reference accuracy or cataloging rules for the year 2001? Want a chance to talk about humorous fiction or to explore the alternate worlds of the science fiction and fantasy genres? Interested in the kinds of continuing education programs most librarians only dream of? If so, it is time for you to do now what we did more than ten years ago and create your own organization to provide stimulating programs to nourish readers' advisors in your area.

In this chapter, we plan to demonstrate how easily you can create an organization that provides ongoing education for readers' services staff. Following the key questions all journalism students learn (who, what, when, where, why, and how), Vivian Mortensen will cover the what—factors to consider in setting up such an organization—and Ted Balcom will discuss how to organize such a group, as well as when and where to meet. First, however, Joyce Saricks will cover the who and the why. The who is easy to define: This organization is for all of us involved in working with fiction collections and readers, whether we already provide readers' advisory or not. The why takes more time to explain.

Part 1: The Adult Reading Round Table

Joyce Saricks

The Adult Reading Round Table grew out of a time when programs for reference and readers' service librarians were primarily oriented toward computers and/or reference tools and techniques. It was a bleak time for those of us who also needed to consider fiction readers in libraries.

Many of us worked with fiction readers in our daily activities at our libraries and we wanted something more; we were desperate for programs that fostered the skills we and our staffs needed to work better with readers. Since no other group seemed interested in providing these programs, we decided we would have to provide them ourselves.

A group of librarians who had worked together on a Read Illinois project in the spring of 1984 met to talk about future programs we could do—and the Adult

Reading Round Table was born. Approximately fifteen interested librarians from three Chicago-area library systems formed the steering committee for this new group and planned our first program. Although that first program wasn't totally successful, all of us who were there saw what these programs could become. We noted three consistent trends:

1. Everyone was overwhelmingly enthusiastic about the focus of the group and wanted more programs about readers' advisory and working with fiction readers.

2. Everyone expressed an interest that still underscores all our activities: programs needed to be practical, covering ideas, authors, techniques attendees could take back to their libraries and use immediately.

3. The wonderful conversation at the dinner table after the meetings has been the focus of comments for more than ten years. People talked about books! It was amazing to see how hungry our fellow librarians were for that basic pleasure.

From these humble beginnings we developed the format of meetings we still follow today with three types of practical programs offered every year:

1. A small group discussion on a theme (All participants bring books and leaders direct each small group discussion.)

2. Nuts and bolts presentations which highlight basic readers' advisory techniques from booktalking to annotation writing and much in between, and

3. Literature studies which allow participants to expand their knowledge of a particular genre.

A network of peers

Important though they are, the programs are only one reason to create such a group. The best reason to form this kind of organization is that it allows us to develop a network of our peers, other readers' advisors, with whom we can share our interests and questions.

Answers to questions about fiction tend to be elusive. It is often almost impossible to use standard reference tools and techniques to follow through on the readers' advisory questions we receive, perhaps to locate that book a patron remembers reading a few months back but cannot find now. He may remember the plot, but even that is not enough if you have not read the book or read about it and remembered the title. For example, at one library a patron was trying to find a book in which a coffin falls off a train. The coffin is wrapped in kudzu and when a farmer discovers it and opens it, a vampire escapes as a lunar moth.

It is often frustrating when a patron remembers so much, but we have few resources to track down the answer. None of us can ever read enough or remember enough to handle all the questions we get. Now these questions are taken to our steering committee meetings or sent to the Adult Reading Round Table newsletter editor. Other readers remember the books and send back answers. (And patrons think we're wonderful! The book, by the way, was *Fiends* by John Farris. A member of the ARRT steering committee had read it.) No reference book will ever provide all these answers. We expand our knowledge through connections with readers' advisors.

Readers' advisors, members of our group, by the way, are not just reference librarians or readers' services librarians. The group includes all levels of staff, professionals and para-professionals, who work with readers and the fiction collection or who have an interest in fiction—from circulation, technical services, and outreach, and even administration.

A readers' advisory interest group provides all librarians who work with fiction readers an opportunity to make contact with their peers, to share ideas for better service, to raise questions, and to share reading suggestions. On a more personal level, we have made more contacts with readers' advisors, more lasting friendships, than we ever did with any other library group. The reason may be that sharing reading interests and talking about books forces us to make contact on a more personal level. Whatever the reason, these are contacts we know we can rely on.

Promoting professional growth

Beyond these important links with librarians who share similar interests, this kind of readers' advisory programming group supplies useful information that promotes our growth as librarians, at general meetings as well as at steering committee meetings. Steering committee meetings can be as stimulating as the general meetings. In addition, since steering committee members are intimately involved in providing readers' advisory, we know the problems we encounter in our jobs and we look to organize practical meetings that will help us as well as the other members.

Lastly, organizing and/or being part of a readers' advisory interest group can give us a kind of political power in our own libraries. Not only can a readers' advisory interest group give us ideas for improving our own readers' advisory service, we can use the example of other librarians, and the kind of special service they provide, to persuade our own libraries that we ought to be doing this too. With a readers' advisory interest group we have a group of librarians and their opinions to support our ideas and activities.

Interest in readers' advisory has mushroomed in the past decade. Once someone in your area starts providing readers' advisory, starts talking with fiction readers about their interests and needs, you will have patrons coming to your desk and asking that you provide the same service. We have all seen this happen. A readers' advisory interest group will give you the resources to start and expand such a service.

If you already have a readers' advisory service in your library, forming and joining such an interest group makes your own service department more creditable. It validates the work you already do. It also gives you ammunition to use with your administration and board, demonstrating that this service is so vital to libraries that a group has been created just to foster further education in this area. This is an argument an administrator will likely find hard to ignore and another validation that your library is providing quality service.

Part 2: Establishing a Readers' Advisory Network

Vivian Mortensen

How do you start a readers' advisory group in your area? What do you need to consider when creating a local network for readers' advisors? Below we have listed points you should consider in setting up such a "support group." These ideas are based on experiences we have had working with the ARRT during its early years. Perhaps you can learn from our experiences—both positive and negative—to develop your own organization.

The steering committee

Although one person can individually create a readers' advisory network, a group effort provides more input and feedback, a base for recruiting members, assistance with the work load, and especially, moral support when things don't run smoothly. Group efforts take organization and meetings, so first you must establish a steering committee to run the organization.

Invite staff from libraries throughout the area you wish to serve to an opening meeting. These people should share an interest in readers' advisory, although they do not have to be working readers' advisors. They can be a blend of professionals and nonprofessionals and can be from a variety of departments, such as reference, circulation, outreach or administration. Try to recruit members with a variety of skills—some who are influential with the library community, some who are organizational whizs, some who have exceptional knowledge of books, or even some who are just dedicated to this idea and willing to spend the extra hours to make phone calls, prepare fliers, research speakers and attend to all the other time consuming duties.

The number of members varies according to the scope of the organization. A small steering committee is more manageable but each member might have to take on more responsibilities. ARRT's steering committee started with eight members but has now grown to nineteen.

When you contact potential members for the steering committee, outline the amount of commitment you expect and have them agree to this in the beginning. You must have members who have the time and dedication to get this organization established.

Steering committee meeting times and locations

Initially it is important to meet monthly. There is much to accomplish and every stage of producing a program should be reviewed by the committee, including creating the flier, choosing the menu and finding the speaker. It is important for a new organization to take the time to polish the details. Later when things have been running smoothly, this is not as crucial.

Set a schedule of steering committee meetings. Make the times, dates and locations simple to remember (such as the first Thursday of every month at one location). Don't waste meeting time deciding where to meet, worrying about who can or cannot come on a particular date, etc. This set schedule also helps when you are recruiting new members who can be told as they join the committee when they are expected to attend meetings and how far they will have to travel to get to them.

Also try to schedule each meeting for a convenient time and limit the length. It's easier to arrange time away from the library if the meetings are short and don't finish at rush hour.

Committee leadership

Once the steering committee meets, set up some committee assignments to provide some organization and prevent misunderstandings. A chairman, a secretary, and a treasurer are essential positions to be established at this opening meeting. These committee assignments can be informally appointed or voted upon by the members.

Other designations can be made at this first meeting or members can volunteer for assignments as workers are needed. These jobs include people to coordinate each program, people to make arrangements for program sites, a person to create and distribute the fliers, a publicity chairman to send out information about the organization and its program, and perhaps a membership chairman.

ARRT's steering committee of nineteen members works well to divide the work load and to create a true working committee. Each member volunteers for a specific task:

Chairman   Schedules the meetings, appoints new members to the steering committee, runs the meetings and oversees the organization.

Secretary   Takes minutes for each meeting and sends out copies to each member of the steering committee.

Treasurer   Writes the checks and presents a financial statement at the steering committee meetings.

Program Coordinators (three)   Each arrange one of the three programs presented annually. Once a program is approved by the steering committee, the program coordinator must supply the speaker and introduce him or her at the program.

Program Arrangers (three)   Work with area restaurants and banquet halls to provide sites for the three programs. They are responsible for registering the program attendees and providing them with name tags at the program.

Program Fliers Chairman   Creates, prints and distributes the fliers for the three programs held annually.

Publicity Chairman   Sends information about the programs and the organization to the library systems within the area.

Membership Chairman   Creates and distributes the membership flier. This position is also responsible for maintaining a membership list and printing labels for the fliers and newsletters.

Bibliography Editor   Coordinates and prints the annual bibliography produced by the steering committee for the membership.

Genre Study Chairman   Leads the bimonthly genre study meetings which are open to the steering committee and the general membership.

Genre Study Secretary   Takes minutes for the genre study meetings and sends out copies to each participant.

Newsletter Editors (three)   Create and produce three newsletters annually which are sent to the general membership.

Notebook Chairman   Maintains bibliographies and adult reading club materials produced by individual members which are kept in notebooks and are loaned to members needing ideas and suggestions.

Size of the organization

One of the first criteria for the steering committee to consider is the area of service for the organization. How wide an expanse should you cover? How far (or more specifically, how many minutes in the car) will potential members drive to a meeting? A larger area will provide more members and thus the potential for greater attendance at meetings and a larger treasury. However, members can refuse to attend if they have to drive too far. But a smaller limit can be costly when the program fees (the fliers, the speaker charges, etc.) are divided among a lower number of attendees.

There are no easy solutions. ARRT has a service base of more than 60 miles in diameter. Annually there are complaints about the long drives to the program locations. We have resolved this problem by hosting the three yearly programs in different locations.

Defining the scope of the organization

The steering committee must set some limits for the organization. Does it cover all types of readers' advisory or is it limited to adult materials? Is it limited to fiction materials? Should the organization include nonprint advisory? Should the focus be only on materials or also on skills to help patrons use these materials? Should the programs incorporate only direct readers' advisory or should they also include indirect methods such as bibliographies or author appearances?

Determining the scope gives the steering committee direction in planning its programming and recruiting its membership. As the organization continues through the years, the guidelines can embrace new ideas and changes in philosophy, but in the beginning, guidelines should be firmly set and followed.

Mission statement

Once you've set some guidelines for your group, write a mission statement. This will set the stage for planning meetings and offering membership to the library community. It will also give purpose and significance to your group in writing—so important these days when the same budget is used for Internet training and computer workshops, and library staff may have to choose which meetings to attend.

The mission statement for ARRT is short and simple:

> *The Adult Reading Round Table consists of those who are interested in developing their readers' advisory skills and in promoting literature and reading for pleasure. Most members work in Chicago area libraries.*

You'll notice that "developing readers' advisory skills" is listed as the primary goal, a goal that members and their supervisors can easily understand and support. You'll also note that both literature and pleasure reading are included—these two items are not always same. The statement also defines the area—who will be recruited to the organization and where the meetings will be held.

Finances

Finances are the next consideration. Who is going to write the checks? Who will pay for the fliers or make a deposit for a restaurant before the first money is received? Who is going to cover losses from a poorly attended program? These are among the questions to think about.

Charging an initial membership fee is an alternative method. Asking for a small amount gives the organization some cash up front. It can be tricky to ask potential members to join your organization before you have proven yourself! But is also gives your group some independence and by counting the number of memberships, the steering committee will have an immediate idea of the size and interest in your group.

Getting Started

When ARRT was established, the Downers Grove Public Library was initially its bank. The library paid for the fliers for the first meeting and made the deposit for the caterers. Once money for the program started coming in, ARRT reimbursed Downers Grove for its expenses. Later an account was set up for the small amount of profit made, again using the resources and tax number of Downers Grove. That first year ARRT ran into a deficit and luckily, Downers Grove paid for the losses until the difference could be recouped. Finding a benefactor to handle your money is one way to work out the financial structure.

A checking account should be set up so that the treasurer can pay the bills. You may need a tax identification number from the state. Your bank representative should be able to help you obtain the forms and arrange these details.

The treasurer should track your funds carefully and give regular financial statements to the steering committee. It is important for the entire committee to be aware of the financial status of the organization. You cannot plan programs without the resources to pay for them.

Publicity considerations

Good publicity takes planning. Arranging great programs means nothing if the library community doesn't know about them. Plan on printing lots of fliers. Although attractive fliers are important, if funds are limited, spend your money on volume, not fancy printing. Distribute the fliers, including the membership brochures, everywhere you can. Send copies to all the libraries in your service area and any other locations, such as library system offices or library schools, where potential members might see the announcement. Try posting information on the Internet or through library system newsletters. Ask steering committee members to announce upcoming programs at meetings where potential members might attend. Don't be reluctant to get the word out about your organization.

The sky is the limit

Successful programs will fire up the steering committee to tackle more projects. ARRT started with only two programs the first year, but now we handle three newsletters each year, an ongoing genre study group, a bibliography produced by the steering committee and presented to the membership for duplication in their libraries, notebooks filled with bibliography ideas and adult summer reading club tips, and special all-day workshops to develop readers' advisory skills. Start small and build on your successes. There are endless projects if you can find members to work on them.

It's not all work...

Although there is much to do to get a readers' advisory organization started, try to keep things simple. Recruit a good steering committee, write a clear mission statement and build a strong publicity network, and your organization should be successful.

Duplicate a program idea that's been effective elsewhere, such as a small group discussion of classics or a program on organizing a book discussion, rather than test a risky idea. If funds are shaky, have the meeting in a library or free meeting space rather than pay a room deposit.

Always remember that the steering committee members should support each other. It's easy to giggle at others' reading tastes or make snide remarks when someone asks a naive question, but setting up a network is designed to help others gain knowledge and confidence. Only by respecting each other will the group grow. Networking, however, is not all work. ARRT members have lots of fun at their meetings. At the steering committee we recommend books to each other, pass on literary gossip and try to answer book searches. During the dinner hour at the programs, we delve into the presentations and find out the latest library news as well as shop talk. This sharing alone is worth the time and effort to establish a group.

Membership fliers

Once the steering committee has made decisions concerning a mission statement, the type of programming to schedule, and the scope of the organization, a membership flier should be produced. This flier should provide general information about the organization and announce upcoming programs. It should also supply the membership requirements and explain any fees needed to belong.

Part 3: Activities of the Adult Reading Round Table

Ted Balcom

This information about the activities of ARRT will, I hope, give you some practical ideas if you develop a similar support group in your area.

As mentioned earlier, ARRT has typically held three program meetings during a year's time. At the beginning of our group's life, we chose to meet in those months that had five Wednesdays—on the fifth Wednesday, thinking that this schedule would not conflict with the regular meetings of other groups and thus give our members the best opportunity to attend. We found that this concept did not always work—for instance, if the months with five Wednesdays were too close to each other, or if other significant library-related events, such as the Illinois Library Association (ILA) or American Library Association (ALA) conferences, had already been scheduled during those months. We also had to be certain that we could find a suitable location for a particular meeting on the date that we had selected for it.

One of the most important considerations for us in determining a location was that to find a place where we could hold the program portion in one area, and then eat our meal together in a different area. This was important to our group because we did not want the restaurant staff setting up for the dinner all around us, while we were having our program. Not all restaurants are equipped with enough space for both a program area and a meal area that are separate, but we have managed to find a few, and of course, once discovered, those are the places to which we have returned.

Finding the right location

We also wanted our locations to be convenient and accessible for our members, and since our membership area is large (the Chicago suburbs—north, west and south), we have tried a couple of methods to appeal to those in the group. One was to always meet at the same place, something fairly central and easy to reach—in our case, it happened to be a country club, with a variety of rooms to choose from, bar facilities, and plenty of free parking. We found this idea to be fairly workable, except that our members got tired of always going to the same place. The environment and the cuisine became predictable. Another problem—sometimes the place was not available when we wanted it. So the other method we used was to look for different places, and each year, to spread the choices around geographically—one north, one south, and one sort of in the middle. If you go this route, once you find your locations, whether they be restaurants, banquet halls, or country clubs, you can repeat them from year to year, which seems to be satisfactory for both the steering committee and the members. You've provided some variety for the members, but you've also established some known quantities for the planners, so that they don't have to keep reinventing the wheel every year.

Another note about scheduling program meetings—we have shied away from meeting during the dead of winter and the dead of summer, thinking that our ability to lure attendees at those times would probably be weakened.

Our routine for the programs has been pretty much the same over the years: meeting in the late afternoon, for a social hour, program, and dinner. Here's the schedule: social hour, 4:30 to 5:00; program, 5:00 to 6:15; break, 6:15 to 6:30; dinner, 6:30 to 8:00. One of the big pluses of this timetable is that members get to network both before and after the program. At dinner, the discussion about the program topic may continue—or members can discuss other related matters, such as books recently read and enjoyed, or new activities taking place in their libraries. And everyone's out in time to get home before nine o'clock—which means something, since after all, tomorrow's another work day!

Program formats

ARRT has a scheme for the topics presented at its three program meetings during the year. As mentioned earlier, three types of programs are offered each year, always the same three types: 1) an hour of small group discussions, which emphasizes member participation; 2) a "nuts and bolts" presentation, which focuses on how to do some aspect of readers' advisory work; and 3) literature or genre study, which examines a specific area in which our readers read actively and which helps us to better understand their needs. The format for the first program— small group discussions—is always the same, with the registrants being assigned to a group at the time they register. When they come to the meeting, their name tag has a number on it, telling them the group to which they have been assigned. The other two programs, "nuts and bolts" and literature study, have had varied formats—either lectures or panel discussions, with questions from the group at the end of the presentations. By the way, the order of the programs changes around—with small group discussions first one year, but then perhaps "nuts and bolts" first the next year, and literature study first the year after that. To some extent, the order seems to depend upon when specific speakers are available.

Finding qualified, interesting presenters is perhaps the biggest challenge in program planning. Many ARRT programs have utilized our own members—either members of the steering committee or others within the group. In some cases, members have volunteered to give programs, and in others, someone within the group has known of another member who could be invited to present a program. When these possibilities have been exhausted, you have to go outside your membership, and this raises a couple of concerns. How do you find someone who is qualified and a good presenter if you've never heard them speak before? And how do you know if you can afford them?

Fees for speakers

At the beginning, the ARRT members presented programs for ARRT for no fee. As ARRT became more successful and built a treasury, we were able to offer program presenters from within the group a free meal and a small honorarium. With speakers from the outside, we felt that we always had to pay for their meal, offer them an honorarium, and perhaps cover other expenses as well. Other expenses might include transportation (airfare or mileage), lodging, and other meals (dinner the night before, breakfast the day of the program).

Also, at the beginning, we tended to rely on our own members to be our presenters because we couldn't afford to go very far afield. Having cash in the bank gives you more flexibility—to offer outside points of view, to provide variety. This is important if you want to maintain membership interest. No one wants to hear the same speakers all the time, no matter how knowledgeable and entertaining they might be.

ARRT has produced a flier that describes many of the programs we've presented over the years. It shows the topics we chose, what formats we used, what presenters we booked. In finding outside presenters, we looked for other librarians who had achieved something of note in regard to readers' advisory in their libraries, such as teachers or professors with special expertise, members of local college or community college faculties, members of ALA's *Booklist* staff, and "fans" (people who were known to be very familiar with a particular genre) who could share some of their knowledge with the group.

If you haven't heard a speaker before and are going with someone else's recommendation, you don't know exactly what you're going to get. So, with an outside or unfamiliar presenter, you must be very specific about what you want, and then hope for the best.

We always try to provide handouts to go with our programs—many members of the group feel that these are the most valuable part of the program! The handouts are sometimes provided by the speaker and other times are the work of members of the steering committee. Steering committee members have usually relied on their home libraries to provide the handouts at no extra cost, but sometimes, if the handouts are especially ambitious, ARRT has offered some reimbursement money.

Developing special programs

ARRT has developed some special, extra programs, too. All-day workshops, where presentations have been given in both the morning and the afternoon, with a luncheon in between. One of these focused on *Genreflecting* and our speaker was the author of that well-known reference tool, Betty Rosenberg, who provided information about a vast number of genres, just as she did in her book. Another looked at "Managing the Fiction Collection," which featured several presenters, including a lecture and a panel discussion, as well as break-out groups for the participants.

Over the years, we have developed programs for ILA—including a book discussion series for attendees that ran three years in succession, as well as repeats of successful programs that we'd first presented in the Chicago suburban area. Some of our members participated in the Public Library Association's "Very Best" workshop on readers' advisory service a few years ago, and have also presented related programs at other PLA and ALA conferences.

We're currently planning our second annual "round-up" for book discussion leaders, where we'll get together to exchange ideas about some titles that have worked well in discussions, and also to share information about those that didn't. As part of this day-long event, we'll be holding a book discussion for librarians, to give the people who normally commit time to preparing for and leading a book discussion a chance to sit back and be a participant. The book we'll be discussing is the recent Pulitzer Prize winner, *The Shipping News*.

The registration cost for the programs has been of great concern to the steering committee. We always wanted to keep the cost affordable, so that we could attract the largest audience. Naturally, the scale of the program sometimes affects the cost of providing it, so the registration cost may have to go up a bit to allow the group to break even. Having several entrees to choose from and having a cash bar available may also impact the cost. When you are dealing with various restaurants, you find that some are more expensive than others. You have to ask yourself: Is it worth it to provide a different location, if it's going to cost the members more?

The value of a newsletter

ARRT publishes a newsletter for its members—putting it together three times a year is a responsibility of the steering committee and receiving it is a membership "perk." Typically we look back at the most recent program we've sponsored and provide a recap for members who were unable to attend. We also share information about new readers' advisory tools and upcoming meetings of particular interest to readers' advisors.

The newsletter gives us a way to further promote readers' advisory and ARRT—to make our members aware of what's happening in the larger world of readers' advisory, and to let them know what's coming up with ARRT and how they can become involved. Sometimes bibliographies put together by ARRT members are included with the newsletter—the small group discussion programs always result in a bibliography, since the participants are asked to bring with them to the program an annotation of the book they've chosen to discuss, and later, these annotations are compiled into a bibliography and shared with the entire ARRT membership. Topics for small group discussions have included "crossover" books—those written for adults that young adults would enjoy, and vice versa; romances; "gentle" reads; and books about family relationships. We also send the newsletter/bibliography to anyone who came to the particular program it reflects, even though they aren't a member of ARRT.

Now, about some of our other projects. For several years, the ARRT steering committee has prepared a special annotated bibliography on a particular topic or genre and has published it on white sheets that can be reproduced at members' local libraries. The idea has been to offer ARRT members some experience in doing bibliography work; to give guidance to others in how bibliographies should be prepared; and to provide a finished bibliography for members to share with their patrons, with a minimum of effort on the members' part. Topics have included "Vietnam War Fiction," "Thought-provoking Novels" (especially useful for planning discussions), and "A Sense of Place," featuring novels where the setting is as important as any character in the book.

A notebook of outstanding bibliographies

Another bibliography project has involved gathering together in a notebook examples of outstanding booklists prepared in the local libraries. ARRT members have shared this notebook, rotating it from one member to another. It's an excellent way to see what others are doing and to discover some inspiring new ideas. The project has become so popular that the steering committee has expanded it into more than one notebook!

Taking off on the same approach is ARRT's new summer reading club idea notebook—copies of reading club promotional materials gathered together in a notebook designed for sharing. As more and more libraries decide to offer summer reading clubs for adults, librarians will need to find many new ways to "do it better," and so ARRT felt this was a great chance to stimulate lagging creativity!

Four years ago, ARRT embarked on a special genre study project. A group composed mostly of steering committee members—but also including some other ARRT members who were interested—has been meeting every other month to study particular genres. The group selects the genre to be studied, then chooses books in the genre to read and discuss. The first genre chosen was science fiction. The group spent two years on that study—and has since explored suspense and romance, identifying benchmark authors and the predominant characteristics and appeal of each genre.

A new project: Bookmark packets

ARRT'S newest project involves the development of bookmark packets—collections of subject-related novels listed on bookmarks that again can be reproduced by members at the local level. These packets will be put together by the steering committee, with each member contributing at least two double-sided bookmarks. With over fifteen people serving on the committee, the final packet may number 30 bookmarks or more. The bookmark packets will be ready for distribution to our members later in the year.

With as many activities as ARRT has offered, there always seems to be room for doing one more, so this line-up—full as it is—will no doubt be expanded in the future. Summoning energy and interest on the part of the members never seems to be a problem—however, finding the extra time to do just one more thing *does* present a challenge!

Historical Fiction

Chapter Five

This chapter is a five-part look at historical fiction. Following each section there is a bibliography of key authors and works from the subgenre. The bibliographies have been written as a guide to the plot, style, and appeal of the writers so that you can better help your patron. They are not intended as patron reading lists. Secondly, the bibliographies are also very selective, focussing on contemporary writers—the ones who are not being reviewed and are on your shelves.

Introduction to historical fiction

Merle Jacob

Exactly what is historical fiction? Is Jane Austen's *Pride and Prejudice* historical? Or what about Charles Dickens' *Oliver Twist* or Nathaniel Hawthorne's *The House of the Seven Gables*? What of Hemingway's *A Farewell to Arms* or Norman Mailer's *The Naked and the Dead*? Well, none of these are historical novels—yes, they are set in 1810 England, 1840 London, 1850 Boston, 1918 Europe, and 1942 South Pacific, but they were written by authors about their own time periods. Austen very beautifully satirized the problems women faced in her society; Dickens showed the misery of industrialization in city life; Hawthorne explored the problems of sin and greed on a family; and both Hemingway and Mailer showed the horrors of war as they affect the men and women involved. All of these authors were writing about a time and a place they lived in and observed. On the other hand, Sir Walter Scott's *Ivanhoe*, Dickens' *A Tale of Two Cities*, James Fennimore Cooper's *The Last of the Mohicans*, Hawthorne's *The Scarlet Letter*, Mark Twain's *The Prince and the Pauper*, Margaret Mitchell's *Gone With the Wind*, and Ken Follett's *Pillars of the Earth* are historical fiction because they were written about a time period in which the author did not live.

Ernest Leisey, in his study of American historical fiction, said, "a historical novel is a novel the action of which is laid in an earlier time"[1]—and that earlier time had to be at least one generation, or 25 to 30 years earlier. Sir Walter Scott felt that there should be at least two generations between the author and the time period he was writing about. For this chapter, the librarians felt the time period had to be at least 50 years prior to the publishing date. We also limited the historicals we wanted to talk about to those written after 1950. We did this to make the subject more manageable.

Understanding what historical fiction attempts to do

The purpose of historical fiction is to make accessible to modern readers a time far distant from their own. The author may do this by dramatizing the impact of public events on individuals (such as Theadore Dreiser's *Sister Carrie*), or he may take a position on a historical controversy involving people who actually lived (such as William Styron's *The Confessions of Nat Turner*). He may fictionalize the biographies of real people (such as Robert Graves' *I, Claudius*), or he may portray fictional characters involved in real events (such as Margaret Mitchell's *Gone With the Wind*). The author may be painstakingly accurate in his portrayal of this earlier time, or the book may only give you the vaguest feeling of the period. The trend in recent years has been for greater accuracy and detail.

It was the historical fiction of the 1930s which started the trend of scrupulous historical research and unconventional interpretations of men and events. Since the 1930s historicals have remained popular—at least one historical novel has reached the bestseller list every year since 1931.

The historical novel has been a staple of the fiction world since Sir Walter Scott's Waverly novels. James Fennimore Cooper's Leatherstocking Tales made the genre wildly popular in the 1820s and 1830s both in America and in Europe. The genre's popularity lessened from 1850 through 1880 but was revived when Lew Wallace wrote *Ben Hur.* From the 1880s to 1914, Wallace set off another period in which the historical novel blossomed. In the 1930s historicals had another rise in popularity when Hervey Allen's *Anthony Adverse* and Margaret Mitchell's *Gone With the Wind* burst onto the bestseller lists.

Why do readers choose historical fiction?

The problem we as librarians have with readers of historical fiction is knowing why they are reading it and what we can give them next. The readers who come in and ask for Toni Morrison's *Beloved* or E.L. Doctrow's *Ragtime* are not asking for an historical novel—they are asking for a best-selling's author most recent book, and they may or may not like historical fiction. For the reader who does read and like historicals, you need to do a very careful readers' advisory interview. Is the patron interested in a specific place, such as China or the American frontier West? Are they interested in a specific time period, such as the medieval period or the Civil War? Besides time and place, are they interested in a specific type of story, such as a romance, adventure, or family saga? Or do they just want a romance and don't care if it is historical or contemporary? To complicate matters the reader may be looking for all of these—an adventure novel set in a specific country and time, such as Jean Auel's *Clan of the Cave Bear.* Added to all of this, is the reader interested in a book with fast or slow pacing, rich characterization or little, real settings and extensive detail or just a vague suggestion of the time period? It is important to find out all of this information so you can begin to recommend a novel that will answer the reader's question, What else is like this?

Another problem you will have is that there are few readers' advisory tools to help you. Only *Dickinson's American Historical Fiction* is devoted solely to this genre. Daniel McGarry's *World Historical Fiction Guide* is excellent, but out of print and out of date. All of the other books on the bibliography have bits and pieces about different aspects of historical fiction. You will need many of these sources plus your own knowledge to help you connect your readers with the historical fiction they want to read.

Notes

1. Leisey, Ernest *The American Historical Novel.* Norman: University of Oklahoma Press, 1950, 1962.

Historical Mysteries

Merle Jacob

If you ask the average mystery reader, What is a historical mystery? they will answer, Sherlock Holmes or Agatha Christie, but they are wrong. Sherlock Homes, in his hat and pipe, crying, "Come Watson, the game's afoot!" was as thoroughly modern in his day as Robert Parker's Spenser is today. Sir Arthur Conan Doyle prided himself on having Holmes use the most up-to-date scientific knowledge available. Agatha Christie's Poirot or Miss Marple seem quaint today, but she was giving a devastatingly accurate picture of English society in the 1920s and 30s. As the decades changed, the settings for Poirot and Miss Marple also were updated. If we use our definition of historical fiction, neither of these authors were writing about a distant time, but Agatha Christie does seem to be the first mystery writer to set a mystery in an historical period. Her knowledge of archaeology from her husband's digs helped her write *Death Comes As the End* in 1944. It was set in Thebes of 2000 B.C., and it was based on manuscripts of the period discovered in the 1920s.

As with historical fiction, an historical mystery must be set at least 50 years prior to its writing. Besides getting the characters, plot, setting, and dialogue accurate to the period, the author has the added difficulty of creating a mystery—usually a murder—in a manner indicative of that time. The further we go back in history, the less we know about how crime was handled and how a mystery would have been solved, so the writer of historical mysteries must be quite inventive, but still keep the story believable.

While Agatha Christie may have been one of the first to write historical mysteries, this type of mystery did not become popular until the 1970s and its popularity has grown steadily. Mystery writers such as Ellis Peters, Anne Perry, and Elizabeth Peters are now bestselling authors and are well known to all mystery readers. Each month new historical mystery writers come on the scene.

The problem with historical mysteries is that few mystery readers come in and ask for them as they ask for hardboiled, psychological, police procedural, or English cozy mysteries. They may ask for Anne Perry or Ellis Peters because they are well known and often reviewed in the *New York Times* or the *Chicago Tribune Bookweek*. If they ask for Perry or Peters, you can probably give them another historical of the same time period, and they may be quite pleased. But will the average mystery reader like them? I think so, and I don't think you'll have to do too much convincing. Mystery readers devour mysteries, and they're always looking for new authors. Readers of the English cozy—or the amateur detective type—will probably like historical mysteries, since they are traditional in tone and emphasize the puzzle element, the plot, and the characters. Authors such as P.C. Doherty, Edward Marston, Leonard Tourney, Robert Lee Hall, Jean Stubbs, and Elliot Roosevelt write this more traditional type of historical mystery. In some of these books, the historical setting is not very authentic or is played down so the reader won't be overwhelmed with historical detail.

A trend toward sex and violence

The newer historical mysteries of the last few years have followed the trends of more violence and sex in all fiction. Donald Thomas, Walter Satterthwait, James Sherburne, Walter Mosley, and Max Allan Collins write in this vein, so your hardboiled lover might enjoy these historical mystery authors.

Some of the books have "crossover" appeal to readers of western adventure novels, since another new trend in mysteries is to blend genres. W. W. Lee and Al Sarranto combine the traditional western genre with a good mystery. Max Allan Collins and James Sherburne combine mystery with adventure.

A fourth trend in the mystery genre has been the rise of the humorous mystery such as those by Robert Barnard or Donald Westlake. This style of historical mystery has also become increasingly tongue-in-cheek—David Ritz, with a stripper as sleuth, and Elizabeth Peters, with her satirical Amelia Peabody, are just two who use humor to tell their story.

Lovers of mysteries can find what they like best about their contemporary mysteries in historical mysteries. By doing a good readers' advisory interview, you can pinpoint what the reader likes and suggest a historical instead. However, be aware that if you suggest a historical and the patron turns up his nose, this reader may be one who just does not like historical fiction in any form.

Will historical mysteries, however, appeal to the readers of straight historical fiction? It depends on what types of historical fiction they like. Lovers of romance will probably not like historical mysteries since there is no love theme in these books. Family saga lovers won't enjoy them because the chronicles of generations aren't in them. Realistic historical readers may find some mysteries to their liking, such as Anne Perry's very realistic Victorian mysteries or Leonard Tourney's mysteries in Elizabethan times. Those who enjoy reading about real historical people or real incidents may like Robert Lee Hall's Ben Franklin, George Baxt and Stuart Kaminsky's use of Hollywood celebrities, or Max Allan Collins' Eliot Ness. P. C. Doherty takes real historical mysteries, such as the man in the iron mask (*The Masked Man*), and writes stories which try to provide a plausible solution. Historical adventure lovers may also find some mysteries to their liking. The key, of course, is finding what the reader likes about historical fiction—the setting, the time, the plotting, the characterization, the pacing—and matching that to a similar type of historical mystery.

Which authors should you recommend?

Who are the historical mystery writers you could recommend? The bibliography I've provided is very selective. I've tried to pick authors who are writing today and a few classic writers who are well known. There are many more authors you can suggest, and Allan J. Hubin's bibliography on crime fiction is the definitive source to check. In the setting index under PAST you will find many more authors listed. But Hubin stops at 1990, so using Neil Barron's *What Do I Read Next* can help you find newer mystery authors.

The ancient time period has become the newest trend in historical mysteries, especially ancient Rome, which is the setting for books by Steven Saylor, Ray Faraday Nelson, and Lindsey Davis. Saylor's books are more authentic in detail, but have a slower pace than Nelson's or Davis'. Robert van Gulik's books set in seventh-century China are based on real Chinese books about Judge Dee, but his updating of the stories is still an acquired taste, and the books are slow reading.

The medieval time period is far and away the most popular; everybody wants to copy Ellis Peters' success with Brother Cadfael. The authors closest to Peters in style and charm are probably newcomers Michael Clynes, with Sir Roger Shallot, and Kate Sedley, with Roger the Chapman, but neither of these writers, as well as Peters, is really authentic. For realism, Edward Marsten and Leonard Tourney, who both write about Elizabethan England, are the authors to suggest to realistic historical readers. I've always enjoyed Tourney—his characters, Matthew and Joan Stock, are very appealing—the feel for the period, the tone, the dialogue are all quite good and the mystery is very engrossing. A new writer with whom I've become fascinated is P.C. Doherty—he has a series character, Hugh Corbett in the England of 1200, and his individual mysteries, such as *The Masked Man*, are spellbinding. In all his mysteries—including the Corbett series—he uses real historical events, and he does it very well.

Breaking away from England is Elizabeth Eyre, who uses medieval Italy and a swashbuckling hero for her mysteries. Adventure fans and those who like the Flashman series might try Sigismondo.

Using real people as sleuths

The Baroque and Romantic period—1650–1820—has attracted only a few writers, and they are quite diverse. Robert Lee Hall and Lillian De La Torre both use real people as their sleuths—Ben Franklin and Sam Johnson respectively. Both are less realistic and more tongue-in-cheek. The books nicely convey the feel of the times, but don't overwhelm with detail. Fans of Elliot Roosevelt might like these books. J.G. Jeffries' books about an early policeman in 1820 London are popular, but their mystery plot is weak. A newcomer, Maan Meyers, has an unusual family as his sleuths—Dutch settlers in 1600s New York —and these books are very realistic and have been well reviewed.

The Victorian era is another very popular time period, and it has the two best-known writers—Anne Perry and Elizabeth Peters—who are extremely different. Perry is realistic; her books are long on authentic detail with the setting very lovingly and carefully rendered. Peters is also authentic when she is discussing archaeology, but the stories and characters are tongue-in-cheek satires. As different as these two writers are, both are very popular. The only author who writes like Peters is Peter Lovesey in his Prince of Wales series. He captures that light, funny tone of Peters. Writers such as Ray Harrison, Julian Symons and Lovesey are all very realistic writers and would be good read-alikes for Perry. Symons' books do not feature a series character and are very literate—regular historical fiction readers might like him very much. Readers of police procedurals will especially enjoy Harrison's Sergeant Bragg and Constable Morton series and John Buxton Hilton's Inspector Brunt series. Classic authors John Dickson Carr and Jean Stubbs write an older form of historical mystery which is slight and not very authentic, but are still captivating mysteries. Both Donald Thomas in *The Ripper's Apprentice* and Walter Satterthwait in *Wilde West* (with Oscar Wilde as sleuth) write more violent and graphic books which deal with serial killers. James Sherburne does for nineteenth-century horse racing what Dick Francis does for twentieth-century horse racing. Readers of Francis might enjoy Sherburne's Patty Moretti series. The books are fast paced, filled with violence, and authentic detail. Adventure and western fans would enjoy W. W. Lee and Al Sarranto's mysteries set in the West. Sarranto is interesting because his hero is an African-American ex-cavalry soldier. Finally, for murder-in-the-library lovers—Miriam Grace Monfredo's novels about a librarian in 1850 New York are realistic in detail. She discussed the women's rights movement in *The Seneca Falls Inheritance* and the underground railroad in *The North Star Conspiracy*.

Enter feisty women detectives

The 1900–1920 time period has drawn only a few authors—Gilliam Linscott and Marian Jackson both feature feisty women sleuths. Linscott keeps her historical setting vague while Jackson tends to give too much detail and slows her mysteries down with it. Richard Grayson is excellent in plot and detail and his Inspector

Gautier will also appeal to police procedural fans. While these three authors are serious in tone, Michael Pearce uses an exotic locale—Egypt—and a light tone to create a very entertaining mystery, which has a very accurate picture of the history, customs, and politics of 1908 Cairo.

The 1920–1950 time period has become one of the hottest new periods in historical mysteries. It has some of the best historical mystery writers. Elliot Roosevelt is one of the best known, but his mysteries are very weak and stilted. George Baxt and Stuart Kaminsky both use real Hollywood celebrities to solve their funny mysteries. Kaminsky's books, featuring Toby Peters have a more authentic feel for the period than Baxt's books. Both authors would appeal to the reader who likes Roosevelt's mysteries. A. E. Eddenden's books set in 1940 Canada, though slight, would also appeal to these same readers. The trend in this time period, however, is toward more violent mysteries. Max Allan Collins' series featuring 1930 and 1940 Chicago with all its gangsters are typical. They are nonstop action and at times, are more adventure than mystery. Paco Ignacio Taibo, a Mexican mystery writer, shows the violence in 1920 Mexico. The two best authors in this period are Jack Gerson and Walter Mosley—both are very authentic and both feature unusual sleuths. Gerson follows Ernest Lohmann, a Berlin police officer from Nazi Germany in the 1930s to London during World War II. His plots are realistic in detail, and the mystery is complex. Walter Mosley portrays Easy Rawlins, an African-American ex-soldier in the Watts section of Los Angeles in 1945. The racist and segregated society Mosley portrays is compelling, and the mysteries are page turners. Both books can be very violent, and both show a very ugly side of this period. Be forewarned that the anti-Semitic and anti-black attitudes of the period are shown, and the characters who express them are not likeable.

You can see there are many historical mysteries in different time periods and different settings, and featuring a variety of different sleuths. Your straight mystery lovers will easily find an historical appealing—whether it's an amateur detective, hardboiled, or police procedural, whether it's slow-paced or fast-paced, whether it's serious or humorous in tone. Whatever they like, there's an historical for them and maybe even one for your straight historical fiction readers. Try one, you might find them addictive—I did!

Historical mysteries bibliography

A selected bibliography of authors by time period

Agatha Christie's *Death Comes As the End* (1944) was one of the first mysteries to be set in the past. In the last twenty years, more writers have been putting their mysteries in historical settings as diverse as thirteenth-century monasteries to nineteenth-century Egypt. Besides creating a mystery story, the writers must create a distant time in a believable way and have the mystery solved in a manner indicative of that time.

Ancient time period

Egypt

Christie, Agatha. *Death Comes As the End*

Typical Christie with complicated plotting and authentic background of Thebes 2000 B.C.

Rome

Davis, Lindsey. (Marcus Didius Falco)

A blend of humor, history, and adventure as agent Falco helps Emperor Vespasian solve his problems. Less mystery and more action.

Nelson, Ray. (Centurian Gaius Hesperian)

>   The setting is good but the mystery is rather obvious.

Saylor, Steven. (Gordianus the Finder)

>   Slower in pace, but authentic detail of Rome in 80 B.C.

China

van Gulik, Robert. (Judge Dee)

>   Modern-type mystery fitted into the manners and period seventh-century China. Good detail, but slow pace of the story makes it an acquired taste.

Medieval and Elizabethan time periods

England

Clynes, Michael. (Sir Roger Shallot)

>   Lusty and humorous tale in Tudor England which is authentic and entertaining.

Doherty, P.C. (Hugh Corbett/also assorted historical mysteries)

>   Using either series character Corbett or different heroes, Doherty uses real incidents of history to depict medieval times very realistically with a well done but serious tone mystery.

Grace, C.L. (Kathryn Swinbrooke)

>   Authentic fifteenth-century Canterbury with an emphasis on women and their roles; Grace is a pseudonym of P.C. Doherty.

Marston, Edward. (Nicholas Bracewell)

>   Elizabethan actors keep the mystery light and funny but with authentic dialogue and setting.

Peters, Ellis. (Brother Cadfael)

>   Best-known medieval character, with good plotting and characterization though not as authentic in setting.

Sedley, Kate. (Roger the Chapman)

>   Interesting main character of itinerant peddler in the twelfth century with good period detail and mystery.

Tourney, Leonard. (Matthew and Joan Stock)

>   Weaves authentic speech, mannerisms, and setting for Elizabethan times with well-crafted mystery and likeable characters.

Italy

Eyre, Elizabeth. (Sigismondo)

>   Swashbuckling character of mercenary-courtier brings medieval Italy alive in fun tales with the feel of the times.

1650-1820 time period

England

Jeffries, J.G. (Jeremy Sturrock)

>   1820 London is vaguely sketched out and the mystery is rather transparent.

Hall, Robert Lee. (Benjamin Franklin)

>   Cute mystery and dialogue with Ben as unflagging and all knowing hero in 1750 London.

De La Torre, Lillian. (Samuel Johnson and James Boswell)

>   Strong on character, setting, and atmosphere of 1750 England using well-known figures but plot is simple; good pastiche.

America

Meyers, Maan. (Tonneman family)

> Follows Dutch Pieter Tonneman in 1660 New York, and then his descendants in 1775 New York with very authentic historical detail.

1840-1900 time period

England

Bastable, Bernard.

> Robert Barnard writes these mysteries which have his usual humor, social satire, and meticulous plotting along with history. Great fun.

Carr, John Dickson. (assorted time periods and characters)

> Earliest historicals have more romance than mystery and most are not very authentic.

Harrison, Ray. (Detective Sgt. Joseph Bragg and Constable Morton)

> Very authentic police procedurals in 1890 London.

Hilton, John Buxton. (Insp. Thomas Brunt)

> Slow-moving and serious depiction of the 1890-1900 English villages with strong emphasis on local customs and lore.

Lovesey, Peter. (Prince of Wales/Sgt. Cribb and Const. Thackery/assorted time periods and characters)

> Very authentic Victorian color and life with outstanding mysteries. Prince of Wales series is more tongue-in-cheek; Sgt. Cribb has a more serious tone.

Perry, Anne. (Insp. Thomas Pitt and Charlotte Pitt/ William Monk)

> Best-known Victorian detective is Pitt and wife Charlotte; slower pacing but they build well to a climax. Very authentic in atmosphere with likable characters.

Peters, Elizabeth. (Amelia Peabody Emerson)

> Very tongue-in-cheek tone with feminist heroine and authentic descriptions of Egyptology. One of the best-known historical writers.

Stubbs, Jean. (Insp. Joseph Lintott)

> Atmosphere of late nineteenth-century London is good as is characterization of Lintott and female protagonists, but the mystery is obvious.

Symons, Julian. (assorted time periods and characters)

> Very serious and literate mysteries which show the hypocrisies of self-consciously moral societies. Mysteries are complex and engrossing though slower paced.

Thomas, Donald. (Insp. Swain and Sgt. Lumley)

> Fast-paced thrillers with lots of Victorian atmosphere but more violent than other Victorian mysteries.

America

Monfredo, Miriam Grace. (Glynis Tryon)

> 1850 New York is portrayed in these intricately plotted and historically vivid mysteries featuring librarian and woman's rights activist Glynis Tryon.

Lee, W.W. (Jefferson Birch)

> The West of 1860 is nicely drawn in a novel that combines both the western and the mystery genres.

Sarranto, Al. (Thomas Mullins)

> 1880 Tuscan is only vaguely sketched but the character of African-American retired soldier Mullins and the problems he faces are well developed. Fast-paced combination of western and mystery.

Satterthwait, Walter.

> 1880 West with real characters such as Oscar Wilde and Baby Doe, but too graphic in sex, violence, and language to be authentic.

Sherburne, James. (Paddy Moretti)

> 1890 America with emphasis on horseracing and sports of the time. Authentic detail and fast pacing with appeal to more hard-boiled mystery lovers.

1900-1920 time period

England

Linscott, Gillian. (Nell Bray)

> Suffragette movement in 1910 is well handled though rest of historical detail is vague.

America

Jackson, Marian J.A. (Abigail Danforth)

> Too much period detail of turn of century slows down plot line.

France

Grayson, Richard. (Insp. Gautier)

> Turn-of-the-century Paris is skillfully drawn in serious police procedurals.

Egypt

Pearce, Michael. (Mamur Zapt)

> 1908 Cairo is accurately evoked in both customs and politics. Witty and light to read.

1920-1950 time period

England

Gerson, Jack. (Ernest Lohmann)

> Former German police detective in exile in London in 1930s and 40s accurately depicts era in complex and involving plots.

America

Baxt, George. (Det. Jacob Singer and celebrities)

> Tongue-in-cheek stories with celebrities as sleuths are silly but fun to read and not very authentic.

Collins, Max Alan. (Elliot Ness/Max Heller)

> Very accurate on Chicago locale in 30s and 40s and on gangster violence. Two different series with hard-boiled appeal.

Eddenden, A.E. (Insp. Albert V. Tretheway)

> Fort York, Canada in 1940s is cute with good characters and plot but little historical detail.

Honing, Donald. (Joe Tinker)

> Baseball world of 1940s skillfully drawn with strong characters and tough action.

Kaminsky, Stuart. (Toby Peters)

> Best-known series using famous characters with hard-boiled detective. Period is less authentic and more of a spoof, witty and fast paced.

Mosley, Walter. (Easy Rawlins)

>   Watts in Los Angeles of 1945 accurately and compellingly depicted with African-American war vet as the hero. Very good mysteries and accurate picture of segregated society.

Ritz, David.

>   Funny stripper heroine in 1945 New York with hard-boiled and violent appeal.

Roosevelt, Elliot. (Eleanor Roosevelt)

>   Well-known author using 1930-1940 Washington and famous politicians. Fluff mysteries but entertaining.

Mexico

Taibo, Paco Ignacio.

>   Mexican writer evokes 1920s regional Mexico. Captures people and feel of place but more interested in politics than mystery.

Realistic Historical Fiction

Debra L. Wordinger

One of the first adult historical fiction books that I remember reading was *Andersonville* by MacKinley Kantor. At the time I was about fourteen. This is a novel that in some ways has much in common with the great Russian novels. First, it is a very large book and I lugged it around for weeks while I read. And secondly, it soon became evident that I needed to keep notes on the characters to keep them straight. For those of you unfamiliar with the book, it is about Andersonville prison, which was a notorious POW camp in Georgia during the Civil War. Most of the characters in the book are soldiers, inmates of the camp. I kept a slip of paper in the book on which I jotted down the characters' names and one or two facts about them: where they were from, or what their professions had been, or possibly their ages. After a while I knew the characters and had to refer to the paper less and less. Then as these men succumbed to disease or starvation or bullets, I started putting a line through the names until very few remained. Clearly, people always had pains, fears, ambitions and longings and, despite tremendous will, they died. People in the past lived as we live and died as we shall die. Reading the very best historical fiction lets you feel the truth of that.

What I look for in realistic historical fiction is a three way balance among plot, character, and setting. A realistic historical novel should have pacing that is slow enough to allow the setting to be developed. By setting I mean more than a listing of archaic tools or detailed descriptions of clothing or mentions of minuets or the Charleston. In fact, a heavy reliance upon minute detail can slow the action too much; a problem I had with *And Ladies of the Club* by Helen Hooven Santmyer. As you read an historical novel you should be able to imagine what it was like to wake up on a cold winter morning without having central heating, what rushes that had been on an Elizabethan floor for six months smelled like, what fear an outbreak of cholera could cause. *The Firedrake's Eye* by Patricia Finney is about a Papist plot to kill Queen Elizabeth I, but in the midst of that novel you can see, hear, feel and, yes, smell Elizabethan London. You can even sometimes taste it. This novel does an excellent job of transporting the reader back four hundred years. Setting also means geographical setting. Not only is 1890 different from 1990, but 1890 Arkansas is different from 1890 Montana. *The Search for Temperance Moon* by Douglas C. Jones is set in Arkansas and the Indian Territory. *Dancing at the*

Rascal Fair by Ivan Doig is about Scottish and Scandinavian immigrants in Montana at roughly the same time, the late nineteenth century. The characters in both novels are proud, stubborn frontier people; but the land, in both geographical and political terms, shapes the novels to such an extent that one plot could not be picked up and placed in the other setting.

Now character. There is nothing more disconcerting than finding modern characters running amok in the wrong century. I have seldom been more disappointed or exasperated by a novel than I was with *High Hearts* by Rita Mae Brown. All the characters—who are delightfully eccentric in Ms. Brown's other novels—struck me as seriously misplaced dressed in long skirts in the middle of the Civil War. On the other hand Miss Love, the milliner in Olive Anne Burns' *Cold Sassy Tree* or Clara Allen of *Lonesome Dove* are strong women who shape their own lives without being anachronisms.

Theme can be an important element in an historical novel. Many of the best writers of historicals include credible reinterpretations of the past. They shed light on earlier instances of prejudice, as in *Jubilee* by Margaret Walker or *Band of Angels* by Robert Penn Warren, both about African-American women in the years before, during, and after the Civil War. A novel can explore the reasons behind wars or elections, as in the novels of Gore Vidal. Or they help us to understand the hardships and joys of our own ordinary ancestors, such as Jessamyn West's Quakers in *The Friendly Persuasion* or the gritty pioneers of A.B. Guthrie's novels.

The March of Time method of storytelling

Many of our patrons like to read about historical figures; a sort of history lesson told in fictional form. When writing about real people, the author faces the dilemma of being accurate in all historically verifiable ways yet making the person come alive and not be simply a wooden cut-out moved from event to event—what I think of as the "March of Time" method of storytelling. Many readers do relish accuracy with a minimum of interpretation. For them I'd recommend Jean Plaidy and Norah Lofts. Both write gracefully, tell a story well, and give enough characterization to make their characters interesting. For livelier interpretation of the European royalty, try Margaret George, who has written about Henry VIII and Mary Queen of Scots. She shows them as rounded, real human beings. Writing about the same period in history is George Garrett. *Death of the Fox*, about Sir Walter Raleigh, and *The Succession*, about Elizabeth I and James I, are colorful, insightful novels written in almost a stream of consciousness style. Both of these authors should appeal to your readers who like a more challenging read.

Hella Haasse and Edith Pargeter write novels with a broader sweep yet still focused on real people and actual events of European history. Mary Renault made ancient Greece her own. Her writing is excellent, her characters complex. Henryk Sienkiewicz, one hundred years ago, wrote large sweeping novels of fifteenth- to seventeenth-century Poland. These have been recently released in a new translation. They depict handsome heroes and strong women.

The American scene

On the American scene we have Gore Vidal and the late Irving Stone. Two men could not have looked at the same events and come up with more divergent assessments. Just compare the portrayal of Mary Todd Lincoln in *Love is Eternal* by Irving Stone to that in *Lincoln* by Gore Vidal. Stone is the champion of a more sympathetic, white-washed view and Vidal, the great debunker. These authors probably will not appeal to the same audience.

The early biographical novels of Howard Fast such as *The Unvanquished* (about George Washington) or the novel, *Citizen Tom Paine,* might appeal to readers of either Vidal or Stone, since his judgements are not uncritical yet they are sympathetic.

Real-life characters add to the effectiveness of a novel

I have my own preferences (three of them) for what I think makes novels about real-life characters better novels. First, if the real-life person is not very well known the reader does not have preconceived opinions. Michael Shaara centered *The Killer Angels*, his novel of Gettysburg, around Joshua Lawrence Chamberlain and James Longstreet. Chamberlain was a soldier known today only to Civil War buffs, and James Longstreet was a Southerner far less well known than Robert E. Lee or other Southern generals, probably because Longstreet survived the war.

My second preference is that there is at least one main character who is not historical. This allows us to see events through another set of eyes. Any interpretation can be attributed to that character, thus letting the author off the hook. Also, that character can have far more freedom of movement and report on events the historical character could not. A very good example of this is *The Queen's War* by Jeanne Mackin, which centers on Eleanor of Aquitaine. However, much of the action is seen from the point of view of two of her personal attendants, both fictional, giving us an opportunity to see the seedier side of twelfth-century France with which Eleanor would not have concerned herself.

My last preference is that the novel cover a short time period, not birth to death. This allows the author space to put in historical color and develop character instead of simply listing events. *The Queen's War* covers only a few months in the life of Eleanor of Aquitaine. *The Killer Angels* only three days of the four years of the American Civil War.

Moving on, one cannot overlook the novels of James Michener. They are great favorites with many readers. The main character of Michener's novels is always "The Land" whether it be Hawaii, Poland, or Colorado. He always starts with its earliest geological beginnings. Events and people sweep across The Land, but The Land is constant. Before taking a trip, people are often encouraged to read the pertinent Michener volume. Another writer of such *big* novels is Edward Rutherford, author of *Sarum* and *Ruska.*

Focusing on fictional protagonists in realistic novels

Some of the best historical fiction is written about people whose births and deaths passed unnoticed, who did not take part in epic events. These people Douglas C. Jones has called "the gritty, ill-fed, hookworm, unlettered, workaday, pray-we-don't-get-cholera common folk." Famous people may make appearances but are not central characters. The main characters are completely fictional or are names that are no more than a footnote in history, such as the soldiers and convicts in Thomas Keneally's *The Playmakers,* about the first English settlers in Australia. The names are all on official records, but nothing more is known of these individuals.

Cecelia Holland is an American author who has written about sixteenth-century Holland in *The Sea Beggars*; nineteenth-century California, *The Bear Flag,* and many other times and places. She writes solid fiction with a balance between plot and character and is a reliable choice. Sticking to English characters but using settings from the British Empire is Joanna Trollope.

Larry McMurtry's *Lonesome Dove* and its sequels *The Streets of Laredo, Anything for Billy* and *Buffalo Girls,* take as their themes the creation of the mythic West. McMurtry tries to destroy some of the myths by showing the cruelty, dirt and poverty. But in doing so, he makes the cowboys, lawmen, and prostitutes seem larger than life simply for surviving such brutality and hardship. McMurtry tells a good story but he doesn't always play straight with the known facts, which may annoy some readers.

With a setting and situation reminiscent of Rolvag and Cather and character and style reminiscent of *Lonesome Dove* is *The Homesman* by Glendon Swarthout. This novel portrays the horrific toll upon women settlers in the Dakota Territory. Another author to recommend is A.B. Guthrie who has similar settings and themes.

Ivan Doig in his novels of Montana ranchers and small businessmen has created characters so real I often want to shake them. Doig has also written about the Pacific Northwest and in *The Sea Runners,* Czarist Alaska; I'd recommend him to those who like Douglas C. Jones.

Anne Rice has written two excellent historicals: *Cry to Heaven,* about the castrati of eighteenth-century Italy, and *Feast of All Saints,* about the free people of color in antebellum New Orleans. In both novels Rice asks, How does a man whom society sees as less than other men prove to himself his own worth? She has created real settings and introduces us to groups of people little known to us today. *Burden of Desire* by Robert McNeil relates the aftermath of a tremendous explosion in Halifax Harbor during World War I, and draws flawed but compassionate characters.

I started with a novel about the Civil War and I'll end with another one. Covering events as tragic as those in Andersonville but with an entirely different feel is *Oldest Living Confederate Widow Tells All* by Allan Gurganus. From her nursing home bed, 99-year-old Lucy Marsden relates the story of her life which includes marriage to a Civil War veteran many years her senior. There are many good things about this novel, although it is long, nearly 700 pages, and not to everyone's taste. The book has a distinctly Southern feel. Lucy rattles on with her story in a rambling, wordy, front porch storytelling style. She could be your grandmother if your grandmother is a strong, witty, rambunctious, impetuous, often wise, often foolish character. Lucy relates her husband's war service, the burning of his family plantation, the many years of her difficult marriage, her happiness and sorrows with her many children. But what is best about Lucy's story is how clearly and strongly she makes the connection between events in the past and their continued effect on the present, and, as in *Andersonville,* makes us realize that people in the past were real people who had an impact on how we live.

Realistic historical fiction bibliography: Authors you should know

Auchincloss, Louis.

> Auchincloss' stories of upper class New Yorkers are not of historical events but of *social* history. Try *Portrait in Brownstone* (New York: McGraw-Hill, 1987) or *The House of Five Talents.*

Bradshaw, Gillian. *The Beacon at Alexandria.* New York: Soho Press, 1994. 376p.

> The far reaches of the crumbling Roman Empire are Bradshaw's chosen settings. She includes plenty of political intrigue and interesting characters, some historic, some not. *The Beacon at Alexandria* and *Imperial Purple* are set in the eastern reaches of the empire.

Brown, Dee.

> Brown's are picaresque, popular tales that take an ironic view of the settling of the West (*Creek Mary's Blood, Killdeer Mountain*) and the Civil War (*Conspiracy of Knaves*).

Doig, Ivan. *Dancing at the Rascal Fair.* New York: HarperCollins, 1988.

> With a trilogy starting in the 1890s with *Dancing at the Rascal Fair,* Doig follows Scottish and Scandinavian immigrants in Montana through three generations. His plots focus on the complicated relationships of family and friendship.

Fast, Howard. *Citizen Tom Paine.* New York: Grove Atlantic, 1987. 352p.

> Fast started with novels of the American Revolution like *Citizen Tom Paine,* but he is best known for his series about the Lavette family that begins with *The Immigrants.* His novels reflect his socialist political views but not to the detriment of good storytelling.

Garrett, George. *Death of the Fox.* New York: Morrow, 1985. 744p.

> Garrett writes about Elizabethan England with a unique, lush style. Every word evokes the character of his protagonist and the color of the area. *Death of the Fox* follows the thoughts of Sir Walter Raleigh during the night before his execution.

Guthrie, A.B., Jr. *The Big Sky.* Cutchogue, NY: Buccaneer Books, 1993.

> Known for his gritty tales of the settling of the West, Guthrie portrays these rough, often uneducated pioneers as real people. Beginning with *The Big Sky,* most of his novels are loosely connected.

Haasse, Hella S. *In a Dark Wood Wandering.* Chicago: Academy Chicago, 1991. 574p. *The Scarlet City,* Chicago: Academy Chicago, 1990. 376p.

> Haasse tells tales of the medieval and Renaissance world's rich and famous. *In a Dark Wood Wandering* is set during the Hundred Year War and *The Scarlet City* takes place in sixteenth-century Italy.

Holland, Cecelia. *The Belt of Gold.* New York: Windsor, 1992. 480p. *The Bear Flag.* 1990. 448p.

> Well-written, dependable stories with a variety of settings are Holland's strengths. Her characters are not as well developed as some other authors' but are still interesting. For two different settings try *The Belt of Gold* (Constantinople, ninth century) and *The Bear Flag* (California, 1840s).

Kantor, MacKinlay.

> Kantor stripped all glamour from war in such novels as *Andersonville* and *Valley Forge.* His characters have depth, and he tells their stories with insight and compassion.

Keneally, Thomas. *Confederates.* New York: HarperCollins, 1987. 448p.

> Keneally is an Australian author who has not limited himself to Australian topics (*The Playmakers*) but also has written about the American Civil War (*Confederates*) and Nazi-occupied Europe (*Schindler's List*). His books have a serious, thoughtful quality.

Llywelyn, Morgan. *Grania.* New York: Ivy Books, 1987. 480p.

> Llywelyn focuses on exciting depictions of the ancient Celts. *Grania* and *The Horse Goddess* have strong female protagonists.

Lofts, Norah. *Gad's Hall.* New York: Fawcett, 1979.

> Lofts centers her stories around specific houses and the families who inhabit them through the years. They have titles like *The Town House* and *Gad's Hall.* Her novels are gracefully written; her characters likable, but a little flat. She also writes biographical novels.

Mackin, Jeanne.

A newer writer who has written about the French Revolution (*The French-woman*) and Eleanor of Aquitaine (*The Queen's War*), Mackin should appeal to those who enjoy complex characters and a touch of politics.

McMurtry, Larry. *Lonesome Dove*. New York: Simon & Schuster, 1985. *The Streets of Laredo*, PB, 1994.

McMurtry breathes new life into rather stock characters. His West is violent but changing. There is a poignancy for the passing of an era although that era was dangerous and often ugly.

Michener, James. *Chesapeake*. New York: Random House, 1978.

His are long novels that offer an sweeping epic story of their specific geographical setting, be it *Chesapeake* or Palestine (*The Source*). Michener's novels show how geography, people, and events shape a land.

Pargeter, Edith. *The Heaven Tree Trilogy*. New York: Warner Books, 1993. 912p.

Employing the medieval settings that she also uses for her Brother Cadfael mysteries (written as Ellis Peters), Pargeter centers on real events and people; she does not dwell on the kings and queens, but on lesser known characters. Her novels are realistic without being too bloody or bleak. *The Heaven Tree Trilogy* has been published in one volume.

Penman, Sharon Kay. *Here Be Dragons*. New York: Ballantine, 1993. 720p.

Penman writes panoramic tales of medieval England and her kings. They are well researched with lots of politics. The writing and characterization are not of the first order, but they are good reads. *Here Be Dragons* begins a trilogy about thirteenth-century England.

Plaidy, Jean.

The numerous biographical novels of Jean Plaidy are easy to follow and quite short, considering the many years and the intricacies of the politics covered. The characters are not very well rounded. Try *Murder Most Royal* about Anne Boleyn or *Victoria Victorious*.

Renault, Mary. *The Last of the Wine*. New York: Random House, 1975.

Renault is a must for any aficionado of the ancient Greeks. The depth of her characters and the immediacy of her stories are unmatched. I recommend *The Persian Boy* and *The Last of the Wine*.

Rice, Anne. *Cry to Heaven*. New York: Ballantine, 1991. *Feast of All Saints*. New York: Ballantine, 1992. 576p.

Cry to Heaven, about the castrati singers of eighteenth-century Italy, and *Feast of All Saints*, about free people of color in antebellum New Orleans, offer views of little known episodes of history. Rice has an eye for detail and concern for individual characters. Female characters tend to be not much more than window dressing.

Rutherford, Edward. *Sarum*. Cutchogue, NY: Buccaneer Books, 1993. *Russka: The Novel of Russia*. New York: Random House, 1992.

His epic novels serve quite the same purpose for England and Russia as do Michener's novels for other parts of the world.

Stone, Irving. *Love Is Eternal*. West Seneca, NY: Ulverscroft, 1976.

A rare interest in famous Americans and, even more rare, their wives, makes Irving Stone very popular. His style is sometimes awkward, especially when it comes to dialogue. His many fans overlook this. *Those Who Love* (John and Abigail Adams) and *Love Is Eternal* (the Lincolns) are two popular titles.

These "good reads" are by authors who don't normally write historical fiction or have published only one novel.

Batchelor, John Calvin. *American Falls*.
Complex characterization, period detail and a feeling of immediacy are the high points in this novel of two spies: one Confederate, one Union.

Burns, Olive Ann. *Cold Sassy Tree*. New York: Dell, 1986.
This is a well-loved story of small town Georgia life at the turn of the century.

Finney, Patricia. *The Firedrake's Eye*. New York: St. Martin's, 1993. 272p.
This novel brings Elizabethan England to life in vivid, raunchy detail. Spies try to foil a Papist plot to murder the Queen.

Gurganus, Allan. *Oldest Living Confederate Widow Tells All*. New York: Ivy Books, 1992.
The Civil War and its aftermath, as told by gregarious 99-year-old Lucy Marsden.

Shaara, Michael. *The Killer Angels*. New York: Random House, 1993. 400p.
The Battle of Gettysburg, as seen by several soldiers from both sides.

Walker, Margaret. *Jubilee*. New York: Bantam, 1984. 432p.
One of the first novels of African-American history to be popularly recognized. The life of Vyry, a slave woman, is followed from the Civil War through Reconstruction.

Swarthout, Glendon.

Swarthout is often classified as a Western writer, but his are more honest, realistic stories of the West, on the order of A.B. Guthrie or Vardis Fisher. I recommend *The Homesman.*

Trollope, Joanna.

Trollope has strong female characters who mature during the course of the novel. Most are set in parts of the old British Empire. *Mistaken Virtues* is set in India, *The Steps of the Sun* in South Africa.

Warren, Robert Penn. *Band of Angels.* Baton Rouge: Louisiana State Univ. Press, 1994. 375p.

Warren used his historical novels to explore issues of character and rights and wrongs. These appeal to readers of well written, thoughtful novels. Try *Band of Angels,* about a young woman who only discovers she is legally a slave (daughter of her father's beloved mistress) upon her father's death.

West, Jessamyn. *The Friendly Persuasion.* Cutchogue, NY: Buccaneer Books, 1982. *The Massacre at Fall Creek.* New York: Harcourt Brace, 1986. 384p.

One of the very few authors to use the Midwest as a setting, West was interested in the relations between people, the development of characters and the joys and disappointments of everyday life. *The Friendly Persuasion, Except for Me and Thee,* and *The Massacre at Fall Creek* are all set in Indiana.

Historical Adventure Fiction

Sharon Karpiel

The Thirteen Gun Salute, by Patrick O'Brian, is the thirteenth in a series of books about two very different men. Jack Aubrey, a highly competent, courageous and much admired captain in the British navy, is ordered to carry a diplomatic delegation to Malay so they might negotiate a treaty that will keep the Sultan from aiding Napoleon's ships. Also sailing with Captain Aubrey is his best friend, Stephen Maturin, the ship's doctor and (unknown to everyone but Aubrey) a cunning intelligence agent. It is Maturin's job to prevent Napoleon's agents from winning the Sultan's goodwill.

Captain Aubrey and Dr. Maturin are interesting characters: totally different kinds of men who, in the course of the series, develop a strong friendship and become a formidable duo. *The Thirteen Gun Salute* ends in a cliffhanger (as do many of the books in the series) that will send readers directly to the shelves to find the next Aubrey and Maturin episode.

My goal when doing readers' advisory is always to find 1.) an author that my patron will like, and 2.) an author that has written a lot of books. This keeps my patron happy for a nice long time, and keeps him from coming back and pestering me too soon. In that regard, for patrons who enjoy historical adventures, books about the British navy during the Napoleonic Wars are a good bet. There are a lot of them! Several of these authors have written lengthy series.

I think of these books as the masculine counterparts to Regency romances. The stories take place in roughly the same time period, and in the case of each genre, there is one originator who set the style for the genre: Georgette Heyer (Regencies) and C.S. Forester (naval adventures). The two genres have their own vocabularies that the reader must learn. And, if you've ever read Regency romances, you know that many of the heroes have recently returned from the Napoleonic Wars. Read these British naval adventures, and you'll learn what those characters were doing "offstage," so to speak. A related series is the very popular one by Bernard Cornwell about Richard Sharpe, who fights Napoleon on land as part of Wellington's army.

Now, if you have patrons who are uncooperative, and simply refuse to be fascinated by Napoleonic battles, there are a few other kinds of adventure tales you can recommend.

What exactly do I mean by an adventure tale? *The Random House Unabridged Dictionary* defines adventure as "an exciting or very unusual experience." Well, most historical novels are about an exciting or unusual experience. Historical romances in particular often contain heaps of adventure. The solving of a historical mystery could be considered an adventure. So how did I choose books to label "Historical Adventures?"

I chose books that have fast-paced, action-filled plots that revolve around some kind of struggle or attempt or journey, rather than around a romance, character development or relationship. These stories often involve some kind of "amazing voyage," "incredible journey," or "grueling trek" "through uncharted wilderness," or "across barren lands." Very few of these stories take place in a city. They have a very physical feel to them, a feeling of motion and geography. And though these journeys might be journeys of the spirit as well, the emphasis is on the physical endeavor. These books center on what people did and how they did it, and only to a lesser extent do these books explore why the characters acted, or how they felt.

Something to look for: Maps

Here's a hint: the easiest way to spot this type of tale is to look for the inclusion of maps somewhere in the book. If on the flyleaf you find a family tree, you're probably headed in the wrong direction.

You may have noticed that most of the books on my bibliography are written by men, about men. There are historical adventures written by and about women, of course, but often these books are romances as much as adventures. This is not to say that adventure stories have no sex in them—remember, these books are by men, and about men. And I will risk sounding sexist and say that some of these books are definitely written with a male audience in mind.

For example, you will find on the second page of my bibliography two books under the heading "A Dash of Humor." The first title is part of George MacDonald Fraser's Flashman series, which is widely regarded as being an excellent parody of adventure fiction, and very funny. However, I would guess that many women will not enjoy the humor in this book. The main character, Harry Flashman, is not only a self-serving liar and cheat, but also a rapist. While I realize that the author is not condoning this behavior, and that Harry Flashman is meant to be a contemptible scoundrel rather than a hero, I just don't find reading about his exploits all that funny.

The Flashman books are somewhat like the kind of book called "picaresque," which chronicles the episodic adventures of a scoundrel, often in a bawdy and satiric manner. So is Thomas Berger's *Little Big Man*, and Dewey Lambdin's British naval series about Alan Lewrie.

There are other characters that are not purely heroic, especially in the books about the great explorers. Henry Morton Stanley, Jack Speke and La Salle are all portrayed as arrogant men, driven to achieve their goals at any cost. They felt immeasurably superior to the native people they used as guides on their journeys, people whom the explorers considered almost disposable.

I'm certainly not suggesting that these aren't entertaining books, or that you should never recommend them to women. When doing readers' advisory work, we never assume a person's reading tastes—we ask. But you should keep in mind that many of these adventure tales are not, in general, "gentle reads." These books are generally written not only from a male point of view, but from the viewpoint of men living decades or centuries ago.

Another characteristic of books about explorations is that many of them are based on true stories. The journeys of men like Stanley, Charles Fremont and La Salle were incredible enough that they need little fictionalizing to make an exciting story. Often these tales are told in the form of journals. Some include excerpts from actual journals, and some are invented journals, as is the book *The Last Voyage*, about Captain Cook.

Another type of historical adventure is the war story. I have not listed many on my bibliography, because if your patrons like this kind of book, it is fairly easy to find using subject headings and *Fiction Catalog*. One warning though: not every story about war is an adventure. *The Killer Angels*, by Michael Shaara, is a wonderful book about the Battle of Gettysburg. However, I would not call it an adventure, because most of the narrative concerns what the characters are thinking and feeling as they prepare for battle.

Books about the West—Increasing in popularity

Another kind of historical adventure that is becoming increasingly popular is the western. Or I should say, "books about the West," because when we hear the term "western" we think of paperback cowboy stories or formulaic genre westerns like those by Zane Grey or Max Brand. And while these are often well-written, exciting stories, they appeal to a limited audience.

But recently we have seen the rise of what are sometimes called "mainstream westerns," or "literary westerns," or "off-trail westerns." What these terms refer to are books about the West that have a more universal appeal: a greater variety of plots, characters and themes. Louis L'Amour was one of the first authors to write this kind of western, and one of the most popular right now is Larry McMurtry. Douglas C. Jones is another writer who has written many books about the West, but few of them about cowboys. Yes, his books are peopled with sheriffs and outlaws, but also with accountants, shopkeepers, women and children. Almost all of the titles on my list could be considered examples of these "new westerns."

Although I like to recommend authors that have written a lot of books, I discovered it was difficult to find authors who wrote many historical adventures (except for those British naval series). What I did find were authors who wrote a lot of adventure tales—some of which were historical, some not. If you have a patron who is mainly looking for an interesting historical background, these authors won't be of much interest to them.

However, if your patron is looking mainly for adventure, regardless of setting, they might like Walter Boyne, whose books about flying are sometimes historical, or Wilbur Smith, who writes stories set in Africa, or Hammond Innes, or Philip McCutchan, who in addition to the Halfhyde British naval series also writes World War II adventures. Even if your patrons like historical adventures, they may be less persnickety in defining an "historical novel" than we have been, and might enjoy World War II adventures like those written by Alistair McLean and Douglas Reeman.

For an Action-Packed Read

Here's the name of the novel that is the most action-packed book I've ever read. It has almost no character development, and so little description of the setting that sometimes the reader isn't sure where in the world the globe-trotting main character is. But if you have a patron that wants lots of adventure, give him *The Road and the Star: A Novel of Low Adventure* by Berkely Mather.

Historical adventure fiction bibliography

Tales of the American West

Cooke, John Byrne. *South of the Border.* New York: Bantam, 1989.

> Perhaps Butch Cassidy didn't die in South America, but returned to the U.S. and... In *The Snowblind Moon,* Cooke tells of the war between whites and Native Americans in Wyoming.

Estleman, Loren D. *Aces and Eights.* New York: Pinnacle, 1981.

> In addition to this book about Bill Hickock, Estleman also wrote *This Old Bill* about Buffalo Bill Cody. Estleman writes many kinds of books and quite a few westerns, including *The Stranglers.*

Garfield, Brian. *Manifest Destiny.* New York: Penzler Books, 1989.

> Twenty-four-year-old Theodore Roosevelt leaves New York City to try ranching in the Dakota Territory, and finds even more adventure than he anticipated. Most of Garfield's books are not historical adventures, but his *Wild Times* is set in the West shortly after the Civil War.

Gordon, Leo V. *Powderkeg.* Navato, Calif.: Presidio Press, 1991.

> When it is falsely reported to President Buchanan that Mormons in Utah have rebelled against the federal government, he sends 3,000 men on a 1,200 mile march to put down the rebellion. Brigham Young hears this, and gives Porter Rockwell an order: stop the federal troops from reaching Salt Lake City—without killing any of them—until negotiators can travel to Washington and back.

Hall, Oakley. *Apaches.* New York: Simon & Schuster, 1986.

> In this book, *Warlock,* and *The Bad Lands,* Hall depicts the colorful characters who made the Old West a legend: outlaws and lawmen, cattlemen, politicians and Native Americans.

Johnston, Terry C. *Cry of the Hawk.* New York: Bantam, 1992.

> Jonah Hook returns from the Civil War to find that his family has been kidnapped and taken west. He uses everything he learned during the war to track them. Johnston has written several series about the West, peopled with mountain men, plainsmen, soldiers and Native Americans.

Jones, Douglas C. *Season of Yellow Leaf.* New York: Holt, Rinehart & Winston, 1983.

> This book and its sequel, *Gone the Dreams and Dancing,* tell the tragic tale of the loss of freedom for the Comanche. Jones is an excellent writer, and his novels illustrate the West from many points of view. *The Barefoot Brigade* and *Elkhorn Tavern* chronicle the respective Civil War experiences of a father and son.

Kelton, Elmer. *Slaughter.* New York: Doubleday, 1992.

> This story, about the battle between buffalo hunters and Native Americans, and *Stand Proud,* a courtroom drama set in the Old West, are just a few of Kelton's popular genre westerns.

Pronzini, Bill. *The Gallows Land.* New York: Walker & Co., 1983.

> Pronzini is an author like Estleman, who writes other types of books as well as westerns, sometimes mixing genres as in this western/mystery set in the Arizona Territory of 1870. Other titles: *The Last Days of Horse-Shy Halloran* and *Quincannon.*

Taylor, Robert Lewis. *The Travels of Jaimie McPheeters.* Garden City, N.Y.: Doubleday, 1958.

> Taylor, an Illinois author, won the Pulitzer Prize for this novel about the adventures of young Jaimie as he accompanies his physician father on a

journey to the gold fields of California. Taylor's other books include *A Roaring in the Wind*.

Adventures at sea

Carlisle, Henry. *Voyage to the First of December.* New York: Putnam, 1972.

> Based on a true story, this book relates the events leading up to the hanging of 18-year-old Midshipman Philip Spencer aboard the U.S. Brig Somers in 1842, and of the dramatic court-martial that followed. Carlisle also wrote *The Jonah Man*, an exciting tale of survival at sea.

Forester, C.S. *Beat to Quarters.* New York: Pinnacle, 1974.

> This is the first of Forester's famous stories about Hornblower, a British naval officer engaged in the war against Napoleon, which has set the standard for other books in the genre.

Kent, Alexander. *Honor This Day.* New York: Putnam, 1988.

> The seventeenth story about Richard Bolitho, a British naval officer whose career spans several decades.

Lambdin, Dewey. *H.M.S. Cockerel.* New York: D.I. Fine, 1995.

> The latest adventure of womanizer Alan Lewrie, who also happens to be a British naval officer.

Mason, F. van Wyck. *Armored Giants.* Boston: Little, Brown, 1980.

> Among the many historicals written by Mason were several naval adventures, including this one about the intrigues surrounding the Confederacy's ironclad Merrimac and the Union's Monitor.

Maynard, Kenneth. *Lamb in Command.* New York: St. Martin's, 1986.

> In the third episode of Matthew Lamb's British naval career he is at last made a captain.

McCutchan, Philip. *Halfhyde and the Fleet Review.* New York: St. Martin's, 1992.

> In addition to many World War II adventure stories, McCutchan has written a very popular naval series set in Victorian times, starring intelligent, capable Lieutenant St. Vincent Halfhyde.

O'Brian, Patrick. *The Truelove.* New York: W.W. Norton, 1992.

> The 15th book in this series continues the adventures of two very different heroes: daring Captain Jack Aubrey of the British navy, and his friend Dr. Stephen Maturin, a cunning intelligence agent.

Parkinson, C. Northcote. *Devil to Pay.* Boston: Houghton Mifflin, 1973.

> The first of six books about Richard Delancey, written by an ardent fan of C.S. Forester.

Stevenson, Janet. *Departure.* San Diego: Harcourt Brace Jovanovich, 1985.

> This truly is a departure: an 1851 sea adventure that features a woman who takes charge of her husband's merchant schooner when he and his first mate fall ill.

Suthren, Victor. *Admiral of Fear.* New York: St. Martin's, 1991.

> In 1742 American Edward Mainwaring serves as a British officer against those pesky Frenchmen.

A dash of humor

Bowen, Peter. *Yellowstone Kelly: Gentleman & Scout.* New York: Bantam, 1990.

> Together with *Kelly Blue* and *Imperial Kelly,* this is an American imitation of

the Flashman Papers. These too are "memoirs," written in the style of a tall tale by another opportunist and unlikely hero.

Fraser, George MacDonald. *Flashman: From the Flashman Papers, 1839–1842.* New York: World Pub., 1969.

> This is the first in a series of "memoirs" by Harry Flashman; a self-serving liar, cheat and coward who nevertheless manages to get himself acclaimed a hero by none other than Queen Victoria.

Explorers and expeditions

Davidson, James West. *Great Heart: The History of a Labrador Adventure.* New York: Viking, 1988.

> A reconstruction of three historic attempts to cross the barrens of Labrador in 1903 and 1905, the last attempt a desperate race between a man and his partner's widow.

Forbath, Peter. *The Last Hero.* New York: Simon & Schuster, 1988.

> Despite opposition, determined to lead an expedition into Africa along a route only he thinks will succeed, Henry Morton Stanley leads eight English officers and 800 native soldiers on a journey that will kill over 500 of his followers.

Hagerfors, Lennart. *The Whales in Lake Tanganyika.* New York: Grove Press, 1989.

> Another account of Henry Morton Stanley's arrogance and willpower, this time on the famous expedition that found the missing Dr. Livingstone.

Hall, Oakley. *The Children of the Sun.* New York: Atheneum, 1983.

> Based on fact but "considerably fictionalized," this is the story of several grueling expeditions led by Spanish conquistadors across the North American continent.

Harrison, William. *Burton and Speke.* New York: St. Martin's, 1982.

> Also based on fact, this is the story of Jack Speke, who joins explorer Richard Francis Burton in his search for the source of the Nile. During the trials of the journey, the fundamental differences in the characters of Speke and Burton eventually lead to each man striking out on his own.

Hoover, Thomas. *The Moghul.* Garden City, N.Y.: Doubleday, 1983.

> Based on the true story of Captain William Hawkins, who was sent by the East India Company to explore the opportunities for trade with India.

Innes, Hammond. *The Last Voyage: Captain Cook's Lost Diary.* New York: Knopf, 1979.

> This "lost diary" is the fictitious yet realistic journal of Captain James Cook, navigator and discoverer, which reveals the personal side of Captain Cook as he sails on his last, fatal voyage.

Nevin, David. *Dream West.* New York: Putnam, 1983.

> John Charles Fremont, "Pathfinder to the West," was the first to map a trail over the Rocky Mountains and into California. This is the story of his career as an explorer, politician and businessman, and also the story of his loyal partner and loving wife, Jessie.

Ransmayr, Christoph. *The Terrors of Ice and Darkness.* New York: Grove Weidenfeld, 1991.

> Ransmayr, a German author, has based his story of the Austro-Hungarian North Pole Expedition of 1873 on the journals, letters and manuscripts of the expedition's officers.

Steelman, Robert. *Call of the Arctic.* New York: Coward-McCann, 1960.

> This details the rigors of several Arctic expeditions undertaken from 1860 to 1873.

Thom, James Alexander. *From Sea to Shining Sea.* New York: Ballantine, 1984.

> In addition to this book about John Clark and his wife, Ann Rogers Clark, Thom also wrote *Follow the River,* the true story of Mary Ingles, who escaped her Shawnee captors and then walked over 1,000 miles through wilderness in order to return home.

Vernon, John. *La Salle.* New York: Viking, 1986.

> La Salle's explorations down the Mississippi and into Texas are related through the fictional letters and journals of La Salle and his admiring yet critical cartographer, Pierre Goupil.

Adventures around the world

Boyne, Walter J. *Trophy for Eagles.* New York: Crown, 1989.

> Most of Boyne's novels about the U.S. Air Force are more contemporary, but this book follows early pilots, including Charles Lindbergh, as they compete for records and prepare for war.

Brown, Dee. *Conspiracy of Knaves.* New York: Holt, 1987.

> Belle Rutledge, an actress recruited as a spy by both a Union officer and a Confederate Colonel, finds herself in the middle of the "Chicago Conspiracy" to free Confederate prisoners of war from Chicago's Camp Douglas.

Bryant, Will. *A Time for Heroes.* New York: St. Martin's, 1987.

> An adventure set in the year 1923, involving a bootlegger, a detective, a widow, her uncle, the U.S. army and the Arizona desert.

Cleary, Jon. *The Golden Sabre.* New York: Morrow, 1981.

> An American engineer, an English governess and her two Russian charges are chased across 1919 Russia after they accidentally kill a general. Cleary has written several other action-filled romantic adventures, including *The Faraway Drums.*

Conley, Robert J. *Nickajack.* New York: Bantam, 1994.

> When the government offered to relocate them, the Cherokee Nation split into those who agreed to go and those who refused. This is the story about one man who was caught in between, with tragic results. Conley, a Native American, has also written a series called *The Real People Saga.*

Cornwell, Bernard. *Rebel.* New York: HarperCollins, 1993.

> Cornwell has written many historical adventures, the most famous of which features Richard Sharpe, an officer (eventually) in Wellington's army. With *Rebel,* and *Copperhead,* Cornwell begins The Starbuck Chronicles, a new series about Nate Starbuck, a Boston man fighting for the Confederacy.

Day, Douglas. *The Prison Notebooks of Ricardo Flores Magon.* New York: Harcourt Brace Jovanovich, 1991.

> Ricardo Flores Magon's journal recounts his adventures with Emiliano Zapata and Pancho Villa in the Mexican Revolution of 1914.

Dunnett, Dorothy. *The Game of Kings.* New York: Putnam, 1961.

> Francis Crawford of Lymond, outlawed as a traitor, is revealed at the end of the game to Dowager Queen Mary de Guise as an agent who has worked on her behalf "with vigour and wit and independence." His swashbuckling adventures are continued in five more novels. Dunnett has also written a

series of books set in the 1400s featuring merchant/banker Nicholas Vander Poele, the first of which is *Niccolo Rising*.

Hennessy, Max. *The Bright Blue Sky*. New York: Atheneum, 1983.

Hennessy, a sailor and pilot, has written many fast-paced military adventure stories. *The Bright Blue Sky* is set during World War I, *The Crimson Wind* describes the fighting against Poncho Villa, and *Soldier of the Queen* takes the reader from the Crimean War to the Zulu Wars.

Houston, James. *Eagle Song: A Novel Based on True Events*. New York: Harcourt Brace Jovanovich, 1982.

In 1803, the captain of an American sailing ship insults a group of Pacific Northwest Indians, and the Indians slaughter all but two of his men. The two survivors live peacefully among the Indians for the next two years, but what began so tragically eventually comes full circle. *Running West*, also based on historical fact, is about a Scotsman who accompanies a band of Cree into uncharted Canadian wilderness to hunt for furs.

Masterton, Graham. *Corroboree*. New York: Morrow, 1986.

To atone for his involvement in the death of an Aborigine servant, Eyre Walker goes on a grueling journey into the mysterious interior of Australia, eventually becoming initiated into an Aboriginal tribe. *Man of Destiny* describes an 1857 attempt to build the first railroad through the Sierra Nevada mountains.

Mather, Berkely. *The Road and the Star*. New York: Scribner, 1965.

In the first 50 pages of this book, Lord Bemforth escapes a trap laid by Cromwell's agents, fights off thieves, rescues a fifteen-year-old prostitute, gets into a bar brawl and is arrested. After that, the action picks up, sweeping Bemforth to South Africa, India, Turkey and back.

McNab, Tom. *Flanagan's Run*. New York: Morrow, 1982.

In 1931, Hugh McPhail travels from Scotland to Los Angeles to join men from all over the world who will be participating in Flanagan's Run, a long distance race from Los Angeles to New York City. Another of McNab's books about running is *The Fast Men*, set in the 1870s.

Riley, Judith Merkle. *A Vision of Light*. New York: Delacorte, 1989.

Because she cannot read or write, Margaret of Ashbury hires a clerk to record her memoirs. As he listens to the story of her life, Brother Gregory cannot decide if he is more shocked by her unconventional views or admiring of her courage in the face of brutality and adversity. In the sequel, *In Pursuit of the Green Lion*, Margaret is widowed, forced to remarry, then travels to France to look for her missing new husband, lost while fighting in the Hundred Years War.

Robson, Lucia St. Clair. *The Tokaido Road: A Novel of Feudal Japan*. New York: Ballantine, 1991.

Lady Asano's father is killed, leaving her without a home and with her father's enemy eager to kill her as well. She assumes a disguise and journeys the Tokaido Road, seeking revenge. This is an elegantly written tale of courage, honor and love.

Sheppard, Stephen. *The Four Hundred*. New York: Summit Books, 1979.

In 1872 four Americans plot to rob the Bank of England.

Smith, Wilbur. *The Burning Shore*. Garden City, N.Y.: Doubleday, 1985.

After her fiancé is killed in World War I, a young woman travels across ocean and desert to join his family. Smith also uses a female protagonist in *Flight of the Falcon* and its sequel, *Men of Men*.

Stevenson, William. *The Ghosts of Africa.* New York: Harcourt Brace Jovanovich, 1980.

> In 1914 the German government planned to allow the British to land troops peacefully in German East Africa, because the Germans did not want their mostly black troops to organize a fight against white men, fearing that all white men would become their target. But Kommandeur Paul Lettow was not about to fall back before the British, and led his native army to become "one of the most dangerous adversaries ever to confound the British."

Vollmann, William T. *The Ice Shirt.* New York: Viking, 1990.

> *The Ice Shirt* and *Fathers and Crows* are the first two volumes in the series *Seven Dreams*, a highly stylized account of North American history, told from many different points of view and beginning with the landing of the Greenlanders.

Watkins, Paul. *In the Blue Light of African Dreams.* Boston: Houghton Mifflin, 1990.

> During WWI Charlie Halifax, an American flying for France, was shot down in flames and badly wounded. Afraid to fly again, he was caught trying to desert and sentenced to twenty years service flying for the French Foreign Legion in Africa. In 1926, after seven years of flying and being forced by his captain to engage in illegal gun running, Halifax is ready to try another escape plan.

Romantic Historical Fiction

Joyce Saricks

Remember all the times you have helped readers looking for historical fiction, and when you have asked them which authors they enjoy reading, they have talked about Marion Chesney, or Rosalind Laker, or perhaps Jude Deveraux's *Knight in Shining Armor*? It may come as a surprise to hear readers tell us these are the historical novels they enjoy—and we may need to quickly revise the titles we were planning to suggest, but we all know there is no point in arguing about whether these books really are historical novels. If readers see them as such—and they do—we have to accept them, too. In this section, I hope to give you a sense of what these readers enjoy about romantic historical novels, as well as historical romances, and authors with whom you might want to become familiar and whom I hope you may even enjoy.

As a fan of historical fiction in general and historical romances in particular, I see several features which set historical romances apart from other historical fiction. First, there seems to be a different feel to these novels. Authors of this subgenre of historical fiction subscribe to a more romantic world view, and readers can often tell the difference in the first few pages. Let me give you an example. Jean Stubbs has an excellent series of four historical novels that chronicle the changes brought about to a small town in Lancashire by the Industrial Revolution in England at the end of the eighteenth century. The first novel begins with a love letter that touches me every time I read it. It is a letter from a farmer to a townswoman, a woman far above his class, offering her the independence of marriage to him and life on his farm as perhaps preferable to life in town with her maiden aunt. The letter establishes the tone of the novel. While the book is filled with accurate historical details, it is also grounded by that romantic mood many readers seek.

What sets these more romantic historical novels apart from others in the genre is the expected emotional involvement of the reader with characters and storylines. Authors construct a mood which pulls readers into the stories and characters. Readers look for this tone, expecting to be drawn in, to identify with characters, and to *experience* these stories in a way in which they may not become involved in other historical fiction.

Secondly, the focus of these novels is primarily on characters, not on the storyline or a particular historical event or time period. The main character is almost always a woman, and the protagonists are generally fictional, although real people from history often play a secondary role. Rosalind Laker peoples her novels with historic figures from kings to artists, but these historical personages and events are there primarily to set her own characters and their stories in the period. Anya Seton writes romantic historical biographies, yet the stories of her real characters read like those of fiction. Readers do not usually care whether these are fictional or real characters, as long as the books have the same tone.

Thirdly, the history in these novels most often provides a backdrop for the characters and their activities. Actual historical events occur in these romantic historical novels, but they are often related, told, rather than meticulously described and experienced. Although these events move the plot forward, they are secondary to the characters and their fates. Characters are usually not active participants in specific events. Battles, for the most part, are off-stage, and even when the protagonist is somehow directly involved, events are filtered through her perceptions rather than realistically described. Events are portrayed, for the most part, without a lot of blood and gore.

Distinguishing between realistic and romantic description

Remember Margaret Mitchell's description of the fall of Atlanta in *Gone With the Wind*? The action is romantically, rather than realistically, described. We are not actually experiencing the death and destruction; we are safe above Atlanta, watching it burn after our harrowing escape.

In fact, in these historical novels we are more likely to see preparations for battles and the aftermath, rather than the military strategies and maneuvers; we see the *effects* of battles on the characters lives, more than the military and political ramifications. Characters more often react to events rather than actually experience them. Remember, these are very personal stories, and historical events are explored to the extent that they affect the characters' lives. The characters, real and fictional, are more important than the events.

Lastly, while historical events may not be of primary importance, the times themselves, a feel for what life was like in this particular historical period, provides a frame which is clearly vital to readers. Painstaking research forms the backbone of all historical fiction, and that fact is no less true in these historical novels with a more romantic tone. Some readers enjoy more historical details, dates, events and facts about the lives of the historical figures. For these, an author like Anya Seton is a good suggestion. Part of Seton's appeal in *Katherine* is the insight into the characters alongside the throne during the time of Edward III.

Details are not always tied to specific events or characters. Background details often constitute a large part of the books, but these are details of clothing, food, daily habits, speech, and customs. For example, Alexandra Ripley's *Charleston* even gives a thorough account of the production of a rice crop from nurturing the seeds through harvest, and including the fact that rice was a staple of the diet at least once a day.

There is a range of detail even within this subgenre of historical fiction. In the more romantic historical novels, readers are more likely to find background details and historical trappings; in the more realistic books, more actual events, real historical personages, and dates. In both cases, however, details are softened by the romantic tone and filtered through the consciousness of the characters.

These romantic historical novels also share characteristics with the realistic historical and historical adventure novels just discussed. As I mentioned, many writers provide interesting insights into real historical figures and events. In *Anna*, Cynthia Harrod-Eagles' sweeping novel of Russia, by discussing politics and dissecting Napoleon's threat to Russia, fictional characters Anne and Kirov offer interesting insights into the emperor's 1812 invasion. From their discussion and the ensuing events, I understood more about the futility of Napoleon's campaign than I ever learned in a history book.

The element of adventure

Adventure is also often an important element of many of these more romantic historical novels. Look at Patricia Veryan's very successful series, *The Golden Chronicles* and *The Jeweled Men*. Adventure and intrigue are every bit as important as the romantic relationships between characters. In fact, I know one woman who, by her own admission, *never* reads romances, but who waits anxiously for each new Veryan novel. Other writers such as Mary Jo Putney and Amanda Quick add large measures of adventure to their rather racy historicals.

In working with readers who say they want to read historical fiction, I ask them to describe books they have enjoyed. If they talk about characters and relationships among characters, these romantic historical novels may be the books for them. It is usually the *mood* of a book and the interplay of characters in relationships, not the historical period, they seek. For the most part, these are not people who are asking what they should read next to understand a particular historical period. Although they may also gain that kind of information, they are more likely looking for novels featuring interesting characters and an impression, rather than an exact account, of the times.

It is important to offer a range of titles and let readers choose what they are in the mood to read, whether it is a selection of historical romances or a group that cuts across all the subgenres discussed here. As we all know, readers who enjoy a particular period will read a wide range of books set in that period, and people who read for literary style or mood will also cross genres to find the kinds of books they enjoy.

Readers enjoy historical fiction because it allows them to immerse themselves in an historical period and to know the kinds of people, real and fictional, who lived then, as well as what they thought and did. A wide range of books provides that enjoyment and satisfaction, historical romances among them.

One of my favorite authors is Jeanne Williams, who wrote novels set in Kansas just after the Civil War. As a native Kansan myself, who grew up on those tall grass prairies, I find these books take me home; they evoke an undeniable pleasure in time and place. In one of her best, *Lady of No Man's Land*, Williams follows a young Scandinavian woman who seeks to make her living as a sewing woman, going from ranch to isolated ranch in Kansas, Oklahoma Territory, and Texas, sewing for the women of the ranch. This was a common practice, and ranchers even had sewing rooms built where the traveling seamstresses would work.

In an afterword, Williams talks of her own research, even of going to a museum ranch to get a feel for the life Kirsten would have led and the conditions under which she worked. The life that women led on ranches becomes real, and we learn a lot about the times in which the book is set: about the lack of law enforcement in the Cherokee Strip, the development of barbed wire, politics (Cleveland was elected during the time), cattle ranching, how a chuck wagon operates, what to do when caught in a blizzard on the open prairie, and about Bat Masterson managing Dodge City. But for me, one of the most evocative and satisfying scenes describes Kirsten looking out the window of the sewing room at one of the ranches and seeing the prairie in all its glory. It is for scenes like that and the feeling they give me that I and many others read romantic historical novels.

Romantic historical fiction bibliography

Compiled by Joyce Saricks and Rebecca Townsend

Bell, Anthea. *The Floral Companion.* New York: St. Martin's, 1989.

> Small Regency-like novels but with more history and less emphasis on romance. Try *The Floral Companion,* which features a young widow and an artist who draws flowers. Includes scenes of wage riots among farm workers.

Belle, Pamela. *Wintercombe.* New York: St. Martin's, 1988.

> Meticulously detailed picture of everyday life in seventeenth-century England, yet appealing for both romance and historical readers. In *Wintercombe,* Puritan Patience must protect her children and their ancestral home which is occupied by Royalists, and help, as well as love, comes from an unlikely source. For readers of Sharon Kay Penmen as well as Anya Seton.

Beverly, Jo. *Lord Wraybourne's Betrothed.* New York: Walker & Co., 1988.

> Regencies that take more care with characters and have more complicated plots. As with Veryan, characters reappear in later books. Start with *Lord Wraybourne's Betrothed.* Beverly also writes larger paperbacks—sexy medieval historical romances.

Chadwick, Elizabeth. *The Wild Hunt.* New York: St. Martin's, 1991.

> Romance and adventure vie with history in these novels of twelfth-century England and Wales. Start with *The Wild Hunt,* in which a marriage of political convenience between heiress Judith of Ravenstow and Lord Guyon blossoms into love despite the odds.

Dolan, Charlotte Louise. *The Unofficial Suitor.* New York: Signet, 1992.

> Elegantly written, often humorous, character-driven Regencies. Fewer parties and more social and moral issues considered. Stock characters, given unusual twists. Try *The Unofficial Suitor.* paperback only.

Drummond, June. *The Unsuitable Miss Pelham.* London: Victor Gollancz, 1990.

> Adventure and even mystery elements add to the depth of these well-written historical novels, set during Regency times.

Dunn, Carola. *Miss Jacobson's Journey.* New York: St. Martin's, 1992.

> Traditional Regency with interesting twists, often some adventure. *Miss Jacobson's Journey* involves transporting gold to British troops on the Continent during the Napoleonic Wars.

Edghill, Rosemary. *Fleeting Fancy.* New York: St. Martin's, 1984 (c1978).

> Morals and mores feature more prominently than romance in this historical novel set during the Regency period. More historical details, not just the mood and feel of the times, but also a satisfying romance.

Gellis, Roberta. *Roselynde.* Boston: Gregg Press, 1984 (c1978).

> Six-volume Roselynde Chronicles cover England in the 12th and 13th Centuries. Carefully researched and filled with details of life and manners, as

well as politics and historical figures. Satisfying historical romances.

Harper, Karen. *Circle of Gold.* New York: Dutton, 1992.

American historical novels with a gentle, romantic tone. Emphasis is on characters in history, whether the French and Indian Wars of *Eden's Gate* or the rural Southerners and the Shakers of *Circle of Gold.* Brings history to life through these rich characters. For readers of Eugenia Price and Elswyth Thane.

Harrod-Eagles, Cynthia. *Anna.* New York: St. Martin's, 1991.

Details of Napoleon's attempt to overrun Russia set this clearly as an historical novel, but the characters and their relationships, romantic and otherwise, add a romantic dimension. *Anna* is the first of the Kirov Saga. Details of dress, architecture, food, and manners abound. For Alexandra Ripley readers.

Jones, Ellen. *The Fatal Crown.* New York: Simon & Schuster, 1991.

Could Stephen and Maud, cousins and twelfth contestants for the English throne, really have been lovers? With Henry Plantagenet (who became Henry II) their son, not Maud's? Rich in historical detail as well as characterization. Romantic story in every sense of the word.

Laker, Rosalind. *The Golden Tulip.* New York: Doubleday, 1991.

Strong sense of place and history. Engaging, if stereotypical, heroines. In *The Golden Tulip* she brings the Dutch art world of Vermeer and his contemporaries to life. Laker readers would also enjoy Anya Seton, Norah Lofts, and Cynthia Harrod-Eagles.

Lide, Mary. *Command of the King.* New York: St. Martin's, 1991.

A dreamy, poetic quality enhances the telling of this story as a young soldier tries to rescue a girl from the perils of the court of Henry VIII and her stepfather's machinations.

Mansfield, Elizabeth. *Matched Pairs.* New York: Jove Books, 1996.

Gentle, light-hearted novels, often with more domestic settings and seldom with villains. *Matched Pairs* pits friends, plighted from birth, against their formidable mothers, who refuse to believe they might not be well-matched.

Porter, Margaret Evans. *Toast of the Town.* New York: Signet, 1993.

Regency romance with more historical detail and a less frivolous tone. Try *Toast of the Town* for a view of the nineteenth-century acting profession—and additional details of plays, theaters, and actors' lives on and off-stage.

Price, Eugenia. *Savannah.* Garden City, NY: Doubleday, 1983.

Settings in the American South. Strong sense of place, details of historical events, romantic characters and tone. For readers of Karen Harper.

Putney, Mary Jo. *Silk and Shadows.* New York: Penguin, 1991.

Author of Regencies as well as longer historical romances. Often racy, with strong adventure elements and a look at social issues. Historical notes at the end firmly set these historical romances in time and place. Try *Silk and Shadows,* the first of a three-book series. Putney readers would also enjoy Amanda Quick's novels.

Ripley, Alexandra. *Charleston.* Garden City, NY: Doubleday, 1981.

Everyday life in tumultuous times and how historical events influence individual lives. Intimate, personal accounts. Reading *Charleston* leaves no doubt why she was selected to write the sequel to *Gone With the Wind.*

Roberson, Jennifer. *Lady of the Forest.* New York: Zebra Books, 1992.

Robin Hood as a love story, seen through Lady Marian's eyes. Life in the less-than-idyllic Medieval England under King John.

Robinson, Suzanne. *Lady Defiant.* New York: Doubleday, 1992.

Interesting, complicated series of Elizabethan romances with interlocking characters. Historical personages, espionage, adventure, humor, romance, and explicit sex. Not to mention relevant literary quotations as chapter headings. *Lady Defiant, Lady Valiant, Lady Hellfire,* and *Lady Gallant.*

Sleton, Anya. *Katherine.* Boston: Houghton Mifflin, 1954.

Uses meticulous historical research to create involving historical novels that are also compelling love stories. Often includes end notes describing research. *Katherine,* an elegant portrayal of Katherine Swynford, mistress of John of Gaunt, is a classic example—and still read and reread. Her fans may enjoy Sharon Kay Penman's *Here Be Dragons,* but they may also find Jeanne Mackin romantic enough for their tastes.

Stubbs, Jean. *By Our Beginnings.* New York: St. Martin's, 1979.

Series of 4 novels set in Lancashire at the start of the Industrial Revolution. Family stories that examine the problems, moral and social, of the times. Start with *By Our Beginnings.* For readers who also enjoy Seton and Harper.

Tetel, Julie. *Sweet Seduction.* Toronto, New York: Harlequin, 1993.

In *Sweet Seduction* the reader gets a mini-course in the issues underlying the War of 1812 and actually witnesses the battles—as well as the slow seduction of American patriot Jane by a man she fears may be the enemy. In paperback only.

Thane, Elswyth. *Dawn's Early Light.* New York: Hawthorn Books, 1993.

Her Williamsburg series follows American history from the War of 1812 to WWII. Family set in midst of real historical events. Comfortable, "old fashioned" novels. For readers of Eugenia Price.

Veryan, Patricia. *Practice to Deceive.* New York: St. Martin's, 1985.

Her *Golden Chronicles* and *Tales of the Jewelled Men* series set a standard across genres. For readers who enjoy interesting, if eccentric, characters, adventure, intrigue, and strong historical settings. Characters reappear in series, across series, and in single novels. Start with *Practice to Deceive.* Her fans also may enjoy Putney and Robinson, although both are racier.

Williams, Jeanne. *No Roof But Heaven.* New York: St. Martin's, 1990.

One of the characters in *Lady of No Man's Land* says, "Good women, when you think about it, civilize the country a lot faster than all the laws in the world." And so they do in Williams' novels, which combine enough details to give a real feel for the period, interesting characters, and a little romance. In *No Roof But Heaven,* a young teacher faces conflicts among ex-Rebel and Union soldiers, ranchers, and farmers, and the newly arrived Mennonite farmers as she tries to set up a school in isolated western Kansas in the 1870's. For readers of Stubbs and Seton.

Wolf, Joan. *The Road to Avalon.* New York: New American Library, 1988.

The story of King Arthur and Morgan, presented as "real" history. No myths or magic, but a compelling, star-crossed romance.

Wooley, Persia. *Child of the Northern Spring.* New York, Poseidon Press, 1987.

A romantic retelling of the Arthurian Legend from Guinevere's point of view. *Queen of the Summer Stars* and *Guinevere* complete the trilogy.

Romantic historical novels, with a little more

Chase, Loretta Lynda. *The Lion's Daughter.* New York: Avon, 1992.

> Writes Regency romances as well as paperback romantic historical adventures. Try *The Lion's Daughter,* set in England and Albania from 1818 for adventure, romance, intrigue, and humor. For readers of Mary Jo Putney and Amanda Quick.

Coulter, Catherine. *The Sherbrooke Bride.* New York: Jove, 1992.

> Brides trilogy. Humor, sex, and adventure as the three members of the family find interesting and acceptable mates. *The Hellion Bride* and *The Heiress Bride* continue the story.

Deveraux, Jude. *A Knight in Shining Armor.* New York: Pocket Books, 1990.

> Responsible for the recent upsurge in interest in time travel romances. Nicholas Stafford, a sixteenth-century knight, rescues Dougless, a twentieth-century lady in distress. She joins him in Elizabethan England, as they attempt to resolve their mutual romantic entanglements.

Erskine, Barbara. *Lady of Hay.* New York: Delacorte, 1986.

> A novel of reincarnation and suspense as Joanna, a twentieth-century British journalist, relives the twelfth-century experiences of Matilda, Lady of Hay, and the men who want to save or destroy her.

Feather, Jane. *Virtue.* New York: Doubleday, 1993.

> Regency background and details of the Battle of Waterloo, frequent and explicit sex, and revenge make this an amusing read. Anyone who enjoys Sidney Sheldon and doesn't mind the historical setting will appreciate the complicated plot. Also for readers of Amanda Quick and Susan Johnson.

Gabaldon, Diana. *Outlander.* New York: Delacorte, 1991.

> From 1945 back to Scotland in 1743, Claire finds herself involved in battles between the clans and the English, married to a fugitive from the English crown, and pursued by a man who is probably her modern day husband's ancestor. Adventure and romance abound. *Dragonfly in Amber, Voyager,* and *Drums of Autumn* continue Claire's adventures.

Johnson, Susan. *Sinful.* New York: Doubleday, 1992.

> Sensual, humorous romps. There are footnotes to authenticate historical details, but read these for adventure and romance.

McNaught, Judith. *Until You.* New York: Pocket Books, 1994.

> Passionate, descriptive sex enters the world of Regency glamour and romance in *Whitney, My Love, Something Wonderful, Almost Heaven,* and especially *Until You.* Read and enjoy them—your patrons have.

Quick, Amanda. *Mistress.* New York: Bantam, 1994.

> First hardcover historical out in 1993. Sexy, humorous, romantic adventures, often featuring bluestockings (educated women). Try *Mistress,* a personal favorite. For readers of McNaught, Putney, Johnson. Quick writes sexy contemporary romances as Jayne Ann Krentz.

Family Sagas

Joyce M. Voss

Although it is a book aimed at the writer of novels, Rhona Martin's slim volume called *Writing Historical Fiction,* has a wealth of information on family sagas. In it she states that "sagas have recently been enjoying a wave of popularity which may or may not ebb." A really good saga, "with characters to whom the reader is reluctant to say goodbye, can be the start of a long a successful career for its author. Ideally a saga needs a background which has not already been over-exploited by other writers and the best and strongest possible characterization. Once established, the story can continue through volume after volume — each, of course, a separate novel — pursuing the careers of family members down through several generations, each of which will bring a subtle change of period and attitude." For good examples of this genre, Martin refers us to the "works of Jean Stubbs, ...and Iris Gower; they have... taken little known backgrounds, brought them to life with flesh and blood human beings, and done very well with them." Also, we should look to the continuous popularity of books by Catherine Cookson.

These three authors have given us glimpses of the people of Lancashire, Wales, and the towns of northern industrialized England. Stubbs documents Lancashire's people and its social history beginning in 1760. She traces the Howarth family, beginning with Ned and his farm. Iris Gower gives us many looks at Welsh society. Each story focuses on a different class. Early Cookson works focus on life in the mining towns. Her later tales show her characters originating in poverty, but we see them struggle and break free from its barriers.

Stubbs, Gower and Cookson write the kind of family sagas most readers want to find, along with those rags-to-riches immigrant and colonial American tales. In the family saga bibliography you will find stories of this nature, but you will also discover some unusual sagas—these will give you a taste of some of the newest sagas to come off the presses. Perhaps these "other" types will appeal to some of your readers. I invite you to taste them and make your own judgments.

In keeping with the more traditional concept of family sagas, it is not surprising to note that there are favorite periods of history that attract saga writers. In the U.S. there seem to be three.

The immigrant family rising to wealth and power over several generations.
- Jeffrey Archer's *Kane and Abel* and its sequel
- Howard Fast's Immigrant series
- *Lotus Land* by Monica Highland

Plantation life in the deep south.
- Gwen Bristow's Plantation series
- Eugenia Price's Savannah Quartet
- Lonnie Coleman's Beulah Land trilogy

History of colonial times to movement westward.
- John Jakes.
- One hundred years of the Cooper and Fowler families in nine books by Janice Holt Giles, beginning with the *Kentuckians.*
- The many Sackett family adventures by Louis L'Amour.

In Britain, it is not so much a period in history as it is a relationship between the classes. There are two popular types:

Landed-family history and relations between aristocrats and servants.
- *Flowers of the Field* and *Flower That's Free* by Sara Harrison.
- Fanny Cradock's *Lorimers of Castle Rising.*

Family of any class or period changing through generations.
•Jean Stubbs' Howarth family

Characteristics of the family saga

In the family saga we have a strong patriarch or matriarch. It is multigenerational involving one or two families, occasionally more. The story will appear in a single volume or will be given a multivolume presentation. If it is a very long story, of course, the major role is usually passed on to other characters in subsequent generations.

The saga's heroes or heroines tend to be stronger, more independent and more dynamic than the average person. The situations in which they find themselves ar often larger than life, but the author has included enough everyday detail to make them both interesting and believable. Historical facts are important and accuracy is essential, but they are still secondary in the family saga. It is the ***characters*** and their interactions that are paramount. It is those relationships that sustain our interest as readers.

Sagas are presented to us in several ways and may have additional dominating characteristics. In relating the rise and/or decline of a family group, we may be given a straightforward story or one told in flashbacks. Additionally there may be an unsolved family mystery (*The Ship's Clock*), or ancient vendetta (*The Original Sin*) with which to deal. Being as involved as they are, sagas usually sport several plot lines and may cast a broad net over both time and place.

Why do we love family sagas? What is the *appeal*?

1. It continues beyond the "happily ever after." We get to see what happens next. Clare Rayner wrote one of my all-time favorite series, the Performers. A theater family and a medical family commingle and the reader does see time after time — generation after generation — what happens after the "happily ever after."

2. We can, through this fiction, experience everyday life plus a broad sweep of history. On the big canvas we know what is going to happen historically, but in the detail of daily life, we are fascinated by how the characters take to changes.

3. Because we are looking at a time before our own we can foresee the results of actions taken by the characters.

4. We experience, in a very personal way, the impact of major historical events on a particular family. We cannot have this experience in real life, so we find the fictional escape fascinating.

5. Other secondary appeal elements might include:

    the simple accident of getting hooked on a series because you happened to pick up one of its volumes.

    enjoying a certain time period

    enjoying a particular type of character.

These last two appeal elements should be of particular interest to the readers' advisor. For example, a reader who liked *A Woman of Our Times* by Rosie Thomas would probably enjoy *Woman's Own* by Robyn Carr.

If a reader is new to sagas, advisors should suggest some established writers for the patron to try. In this way you will know that it is the type of saga the patron likes or does not like as opposed to the reader being swayed by a writing style.

Saga's popularity dates back to the Forsytes and Jalna

The saga as we know it today gained popularity in the first half of the twentieth century. John Galsworthy's *Forsyte Saga* was one of the first contemporary sagas. In the 1930s, Mazo De la Roche began producing the Jalna series about the Whiteoak family of Canada. This tale begins in 1850. Concurrently Hugh Walpole began the Herries tetralogy, covering two hundred years from the Georgian period to the 1930s. (It's been suggested that Poldark fans would probably like this tetralogy.)

Some of the more contemporary writers who were early family saga writers are Clare Rayner, Colleen McCullough and her "infamous" *Thorn Birds*, Rosalind Laker and her Waywyck books, and Susan Howatch, who made the Van Zales, a banking clan, known to all in *The Rich are Different* and *The Sins of the Father.*

Lastly let me talk of the "corporate creation." A publisher gets an idea for a series that he thinks will be popular. A writer or group of writers is needed to execute the project. An author is contracted to write the books. Here are some very popular books that have come to us that way:

Wagons West series by Dana Fuller Ross (at least 40 by now).

Colonization of America/White Indian series by Donald Clayton Porter

The **Australian** series was written by a woman under the name of William Stuart Long. Her last title in the series, *Empire Builders*, was completed after her death by another writer. Subsequent volumes have been added since then by other authors. For the greatest satisfaction these books should be read in order.

Kent Family Chronicles by John Jakes

People of the Fire (1991), *People of the Earth* (1992), and *People of the River* (1993) by Michael W. Gear.

We can conclude then that family sagas come in all sizes, periods, and with a wide variety of characters. Because of the diverse plot lines found in most sagas, there seems to be something for everyone. Sagas will attract a large and varied group of readers.

As a child I always enjoyed stories about long ago and far away. I loved historical tales. I even majored in history in college and ended up teaching it for a short while. But I will agree with many of you who feel that there's a lot of really boring stuff out there. So pursuing this line of thought a little further, I began to realize that my first requirement with any book is there be a good story. It seems I have found a lot of those good stories in historical fiction. I have always loved to know and understand why people do what they do, and I can't think of a better place to indulge that curiosity than in the kinds of books we have been talking about today. So look those titles over, and chances are, you will find many more than one to take you to long ago and faraway.

Family saga bibliography

Listed below are family sagas, either in a single volume or in a series, reviewed for this chapter. Many of them are current. As with other genres, a reader does not usually like them all. Some are very romantic; others reek with intrigue. Some give us lots of juicy history, usually in a painless way. Others truly concentrate on chronicling a family.

They are grouped by certain appeal elements, but other combinations of these titles are possible, depending, as always, on what the reader finds attractive in a book.

Large sweeps of history

Anand, Valerie. Bridges Over Time saga. New York: St. Martin's, 1994. 384p. (*Proud Villiens.* 1992. 310p.; *Ruthless Yeoman.* 1993. 342p.)

> Villiens equals slaves. Anand presents the mix of Norse and Norman cultures and the story moves briskly from one generation to another. Not for the reader who wants a book with strong characterization.

Halter, Marek. *Book of Abraham.* New York: Holt, 1986. 722p.; *Children of Abraham.* New York: Arcade, c1990. 377p.

> The first volume covers a hundred generations of one Jewish family (A.D. 70 –1943); the second leads us into today. From the fifteenth century based on the author's family records. Many long narrative passages, but still an interesting read. Characters are ordinary people revealed against a background of many great events. A learning experience.

Martin, William. *Cape Cod.* New York: Warner Books, 1991. 652p.

> Two bitterly antagonistic families from Pilgrim days to modern times. Chapters alternate between past and present; the chapters set in the past capture the speech and conversation style of those years. Religious and political skirmishes. Risky love, as the feuding families at times intermarry. As the author does in *Back Bay*, there is a mystery to discover—it keeps the reader going.

Zaroulis, Nancy. *Massachusetts.* New York: Fawcett Columbine, 1991. 709p.

> Zaroulis tells the Revells family history by recounting the history of their state, taking the reader from the Mayflower to the contemporary effort of saving Walden Pond. One of the characters is an "Indian" at the Boston Tea Party. The reader is treated to many important historical happenings: witch trials, factory system, etc. For those who don't want the story to end!

An Elizabethan tangle

Birkhead, Margaret. *Trust and Treason*, New York: St. Martin's, 1989. 383p.

> Tightly written, but comfortable. Novel is divided into two parts: 1558-1578 and 1584-1585. A member of the Woodfall family of Sussex marries into a Catholic family on the Scottish border. This leads in years to come to the question of treason. Included is a friendship with a future queen, a half sister whose mother was burned at the stake, and a feud between brothers. Lots of historical detail.

The English family up and through the World War II years

Cradock, Fanny. The Family at Castle Rising. *The Lormes of Castle Rising* (New York: Saturday Review, 1976); *Shadows Over Castle Rising* (New York: Dutton, 1977); *War Comes to Castle Rising* (New York: Dutton, 1978); *Wind of Change at Castle Rising* (New York: Dutton, 1979).

> The Lormes have an 800-year history as they come into the twentieth century, 40 family members and 50 or so servants. A leisurely read, reminiscent of *Upstairs/Downstairs.*

Howard, Elizabeth Jane. Cazalet Family trilogy. (1. *The Light Years*, 1991. 448p.; 2. *Marking Time*, 1994. 512p.; 3. Not yet published.)

> A middle class English family set against an authentic background, but the impact of any historical event on the individual character is what makes the story move. Smooth reading and definitely for the characterization lover.

Japanese family sagas

Freedman, Nancy. *The Seventh Stone.* NAL-Dutton, 1992. 384p.

> Fifty years of war and peace with four generations of the Sanagowa family

beginning in World War II. Second generation Noboru, idealistic, loving and noble, becomes a Kamikaze pilot. His son, born after his death, has none of the altruism of the father. He demonstrates a twisted patriotism by passionately seeking revenge. Ten years in the writing, Freedman's novel delicately handles the subtleties of Japanese life and speech. Fascinating.

Kata, Elizabeth. *Kagami*. New York: Ballantine, 1992. 550p.

Kagami is a sacred mirror used to examine one's soul/reflect on one's life. The novel depicts the effects of change and conflict on three families from the coming of Commodore Perry to 1923. It begins with a full picture of isolated Japan, so what follows is believable. Wonderfully readable—you seem to be there!

The land and its influence on strong women

Gavin, Catherine. *Sunset Dream*. New York: St. Martin's, 1984. 631p.

Chronicle of the powerful Estrata family from 1846, when brothers fight on opposite sides in a war over the California territory, to 1941. Two of its women will be actresses, and through them is seen the rise of the movie industry. The writing is a nice mix of narrative and dialog. A smooth read.

Wood, Barbara. *Green City in the Sun*. New York: Random House, 1988. 699p.

A mix of history, romance and intrigue. Two families fight over the same patch of land in Kenya. Beginning in 1917, Grace, a doctor from the new English family, and Wachera, an African medicine woman conflict. Some say that Wood uses too many medical terms, but most readers will skip over the terms and read her tale for the pleasure of a story well told.

Strong American ladies

Carr, Robyn. *Woman's Own*. New York: St. Martin's, 1990. 425p.

Nineteenth-century Philadelphia. Carr is known for "her strong heroines, whose pride and independence are sources of that inner strength they must exhibit to overcome the obstacles thrown against them." (*Historical & Romance Writers*). Thus, are the Armstrong women! Riches to rags to riches. Just enough detail of style, etc., not to get in the way of the story. Emotionally involving.

Shreve, Susan Richards. *Daughters of the New World*. New York: Doubleday, 1991. 471p.

The claims family makes on us and the sense of history we have with those non-family members known since we were young are both strong themes. Experiencing Wisconsin, in the nineteenth century, to mid-twentieth-century New York and D.C., Shreve gives each period its due. Rich characters, one of whom disguises herself as a male photographer, enabling her to enter the European war zone, and smooth writing make this a favorite.

History/Mystery/Saga

Gabriel, Marius. *The Original Sin*. New York: Bantam, 1992. 654p.

Reads like a Sidney Sheldon novel. A heroin addicted daughter, Eden, is kidnapped and her divorced mother, Mercedes, is asked for a ten-million-dollar ransom. Mercedes has ties in Spain and some terrible memories from pre- Spanish Civil War days. These play a part in the kidnapping. Eden has been a very spoiled and ignored child, but now she may die from her addiction if not rescued in time.

Rae, Catherine M. *The Ship's Clock*. New York: St. Martin's, 1993. 208p.

Chronicles three generations of a New York family which suffers a curse. As a young man, the patriarch stole a precious clock from his father, ran away to America, and changed his identity. Good fortune soon turns to bad. Told from the grandchildren's points of view, this nicely paced, intriguing tale will appeal to the mystery fan.

Cultural identity

Conde, Maryse. *Tree of Life: A Novel of the Caribbean.* New York: Ballantine, 1992. 384p.

> The struggles of the Louis family against poverty and racism are set against historical events like the Panama Canal, the career of Malcom X, and the death of Stalin. Coco, a contemporary "Louis," narrates, following the loves, laughter and hard times of the clan from Guadeloupe to Harlem and from Paris to Haiti. Impressive writing about a culture unfamiliar to many.

Lee, Skye. *Disappearing Moon Cafe.* Seattle: Seal Press Feminist, 1991. 273p.

> The story of four generations of the Wong family, beginning in 1892, is pieced together by a present day member. Moving back and forth between China and Canada, the tale uncovers secrets, shows the struggle for identity, relates intermarriages, and ponders the impact of the 1923 Chinese Exclusion Act. Some readers may find the story a bit confusing, but with some attention readers will be rewarded. For those who enjoyed the novels of Amy Tan or Maxine Hong Kingston.

Non-traditional narratives as sagas

Thorpe, Adam. *Ulverton.* New York: Farrar Straus Giroux, 1992. 390p.

> A history of Ulverton from 1650 to 1988 is given in twelve time frames in as many different years. Each has a different voice and different type of writing such as diaries, letters, a drunken pub scene, etc. The saga of this English village is complex, brutal, and bleak. Norah Lofts' *Wayside Tavern* uses this same technique, although it is not quite so dark.

Yehoshua, A.B. *Mr. Mani.* New York: Harcourt Brace, 1993. 350p.

> Five one-sided conversations occurring between 1848 and 1982 make up this novel. In 1848 the first Mani comes to Jerusalem. The ensuing years tell of exile and/or periodic return of five other family members. Both family and non-family members do the "talking." The book was originally written in Hebrew. Not for the reader who wants a linear story.

Saga with a taste of fantasy/myth

Bayer, Valerie Townsend. *City of Childhood.* New York: St. Martin's, 1992. 308p. *Metaphysics of Sex.* New York: St. Martin's, 1992. 384p.

> These are the first two books in a proposed "Marlborough Gardens" tetralogy. It's been called a darker version of the Forsyte Saga and uses a technique seen in Byatt's *Possession.* Not a "Father Knows Best" series, the titles should be read in order for greater understanding.

Richler, Mordecai. *Solomon Gursky Was Here.* New York: Knopf, 1990. 413p.

> Unlucky in love with a Gursky woman, Moses Berger becomes the biographer of that wealthy, powerful "mad" Jewish family of Montreal. An arctic expedition (resulting in an Inuit Gursky), bootlegging, larceny and other depravities of the family are related with humor, exaggeration and some darkness. An esteemed writer gives rich characters and a circus of a story.

One hundred years of country music

Smith, Lee. *Devil's Dream.* New York: Ballantine, 1992. 368p.

> Follow the Bailey clan and its music: Baptist hymns, Appalachian ballads, hillbilly, rockabilly, the Nashville sound and traditional music. Each charac-

ter tells his own story, incorporating speech patterns of that place and time *Library Journal* calls it "warm, amusing and moving."

Very romantic sagas

Adamson, Yvonne. *Bridey's Mountain*, New York: Delacorte, 1993. 613p.

> Four generations of women who struggle to keep a mountain. From Morna, a young Irish woman who plays piano in a brothel, to her great granddaughter Ariana, a struggling student with a birthmark, none will relinquish the mountain—even if it means losing true love. Wonderful descriptions—like eating a sundae!

Ellis, Julie. *A Daughter's Promise*, New York: Morrow, 1988. 470p.

> Jacob Roth is the innocent victim of an anti-Semitic lynch mob in a small Georgia city. The incident will drive his two daughters and eventually a granddaughter to life choices pursuing justice. Going at express train pace, the story moves from the end of World War I through the McCarthy era, and this rags-to-riches soap opera will delight an army of readers.

Wilson, T.R. *Beauty for Ashes*, New York: St. Martin's, 1992. 320p.

> First of a proposed trilogy. This entry follows a class straddling English family from 1877 to the end of World War I. The shopgirls' life, the Queen's 50th Jubilee, and the impact of war on the homefront are incorporated in this easy-to read novel. Physically, the book is small in size and has small print.

Contemporary approach to the family saga

Drinkard, Michael. *Disobedience*, New York: Norton, 1993. 320p.

> This "wise guy" novel reveals a dysfunctional California family over five generations. Done in flashbacks, the record of this wacky orange grove owning family is definitely not a mainstream saga. Bizarre.

Levin, Michael. *Alive and Kicking*, Simon & Schuster, 1993. 368p.

> "To live is to litigate!" This could be the motto of this Manhattan family whose various members continue to take one another to court over money. Mostly in the present, the story unfolds through Amelia Vanderbilt, a young trust officer who tries to sort out this family's mess. A wicked and funny story with a touch of romance.

Some books recently "discovered"

Cocquyt, Katherine Marie. *The Celtic Heart*. St. Paul, Minn.:Llewellyn, 1994. 592p.

Cooper, J. California. *In Search of Satisfaction*. New York: Doubleday, 1994.

Dawson, Carol. *Body of Knowledge*. Chapel Hill, NC: Algonquin, 1994.

Gibbons, Kaye. *Charms for the Easy Life*. New York: Putnam, 1993. 254p.

> Told in the present day, but many reflections of Charlie Kate, an outspoken midwife and doctor (not licensed) who is adored by her granddaughter and tolerated by her daughter. Warm, delightful tale related in silky language.

Jekel, Pamela. *Deepwater: A Novel of the Carolinas*. New York: Zebra, 1994. 491p.

> Beginning with early colonization, four generations of a strong Southern family sweep you through the South's rise and fall. Very readable.

Laxalt, Robert. *Basque Hotel*. Reno: Univ. of Nevada Press, 1993. 136p. *Child of the Holy Ghost*. Reno: Univ. of Nevada Press, 1992. 176p. *Governor's Mansion*. Reno: Univ. of Nevada Press, 1994. 200p.

> Immigrant family, suffering from shame and forced flight, determines to gain respect in America. Collision between traditions and American culture, politics and the underworld.

Mahfouz, Naguib. *The Harafish.* New York: Doubleday, 1994. 406p.

> Through many generations, the family continues, amassing and losing large fortunes and exhibiting all the depravity and goodness humans are capable of. One generation produces Nagi, who restores the family name to its proper place.

Mayerson, Evelyn Wilde. *Miami: A Saga.* New York: Dutton, 1994. 450p.

> From post-Civil War to Hurricane Andrew in 1992, five generations of five families take the reader to every level of society in this international city. Hold on to your hat!!!

Parker, Robert B. *All Our Yesterdays.* New York: Delacorte, 1994. 416p.

Rose, Marcia. *Like Mother, Like Daughter.* New York: Ballantine, 1994. 448p.

> Historical detail enhances this tale. Leah, a Russian Jew who escapes the Triangle Shirt Factory fire in 1910, becomes a journalist and lives a "free" life in Greenwich Village. Her daughter and granddaughter take us through World War I and the 1950s. Good storytelling.

Urquhart, Jane. *Away.* New York: Viking Penguin, 1994. 356p.

> Shades of Irish storytelling. Fantasy-concept.

Windle, Janice Woods. *True Women.* New York: Putnam, 1994. 464p.

> From the Alamo to World War II. Based on the author's roots.

Fantasy Fiction

Chapter Six

Georgine N. Olson

This chapter is designed as an introduction to the fantasy genre for readers' advisors who do not (yet!) regularly read in this genre. It is divided into three sections: 1) an introduction to the genre and its readers, 2) a short "Fantasy 101" bibliography of classic titles in the genre, and 3) a list of fantasy genre read-alikes that might be palatable to dyed-in-the-wool non-fantasy readers. Please note that titles of individual books are printed in *italics*; series are in **bold** print.

Key criteria for fantasy fiction

For a non-reader of the fantasy genre, one of the most helpful keys is some way to decide what makes a fantasy a fantasy and not something else. There are lots of definitions, but, to my mind, there are two key criteria. The first is magic, and the second is the protagonist's dilemma.

Watch for these key fantasy criteria: Magic and the protagonist's dilemma.

First and foremost, some form of magic is an integral part of the milieu of the tale. The magic is consistent and it conforms to its own, believable rules of logic. It is possible that the magic presented is a "wild magic" which does not seem to have any logic. For instance, in Piers Anthony's first **Xanth** book, the main character was a person around whom no magic would take place. However, magic was an integral part of life in that society. The fact that no magic could take place around this character as it did for everyone else is what made this individual and his problems unique. In time travel fantasy, the magic is what enables the protagonist to get from this world, *this* time to that world, *that* time. When the author is truly knowledgeable about the history and culture to which the protagonist travels, the world traveled to and the times traveled to are presented with a great deal of realism and authenticity. A good example of this is the eighteenth-century Scotland to which Diana Gabaldon transports her post-World War II nurse in *Outlander.*

Second, the protagonist in a fantasy is faced with a problem, is forced to make an ethical and moral choice, and then act on that choice. In many a fantasy, the hero is an unlikely and unwilling one, one who didn't know he or she was going to become a key player in what is happening. It's not unusual to have a hero who is dragged into a situation, rebels at first, then makes a choice, thinking, "I must be nuts, but I am going do that which is right and true, even though it might cost me a great deal, because there is no one else to do it. I really don't know why I'm stuck with doing it, but I am. So, here I am, and I will just have to do the best I can." This is probably part of the appeal of fantasy to many readers: very ordinary people are thrown into very extraordinary situations and try to rise to the challenge—not always succeeding.

If you read fantasy, fantasy reviews, or the blurbs on fantasy books, you'll become aware of the number of times the words "light and dark," "good vs evil" and "quest" show up in the annotations. Protagonists have made their choices; now they must act. A main character may have a character flaw that leads to wrong choices—choices for which friends and fellow travellers in the venture will pay dearly. If you read C.S. Lewis's classic children's series about **Narnia**, you know that a key, beloved character makes a truly terrible choice for which everyone else has to pay.

> In the **Narnia** books, all comes out well in the end. That doesn't always happen in adult fantasy.

Fantasy as an outgrowth of fairy tales and folklore

Fantasy, in the form of fairy tales or folklore or myth, is one of the very first fictions to which we consciously introduce our children. We should not be surprised that some readers will choose to stay and grow with the genre rather than "grow up" and become "too big" to read "that stuff." Several authors in the bibliography at the end of the chapter have written picture books, especially versions of fairy tales, myths and fantasies (Cooper, LeGuin, McKinley). It would be an interesting exercise to take this chapter's bibliography to a children's catalog or your local automated database and see how many names do show up in children's as well as adult collections. In addition, many fantasy authors began as writers of children's books (Cooper, Lewis, McKinley). There are some authors that move back and forth between writing children's and adult materials (LeGuin, Norton, Wrede, and especially, Yolen). There are even fantasy series where the first titles were published as children's books and later titles were published as adult books (Norton, Gregorian).

At the 1994 Illinois Library Association Conference's Children's/Youth Author Breakfast, author Patricia Wrede said that she didn't consciously write for children or young adults when she was writing her novels. It was when her editor or her publisher read her manuscripts that they said, "This is a children's book," or "This is a young adult book," or "This is an adult book." To her mind there wasn't much difference in what she was doing—she was simply telling a story. It was her publisher who decided how to market the books. Please note, that, similar to romance authors, fantasy authors want you to know they have absolutely no control over the cover art on their books! That, too, is a publisher's marketing decision.

Readers of fantasy aren't too tied to suggested age or reading levels. My son read his first fantasy when he was in the fifth grade. It was *Sword of Shannara*, which is a nice, thick "adult" book. He had never read anything more than a thin children's novel. When he turned in his book report, the teacher indicated that she didn't believe he'd read the book. It was one of those times when mother went to school and said, "Yes, indeed, I gave it to him; we talked about it, and yes, he read it!" That was the book that really opened his eyes to the world of pleasure reading.

Generally, if you read a bit in the genre and get a *feel* for some of the authors—and if you read book blurbs and reviews carefully—you're not going to be sandbagged by recommending a title that some parents might think is a tad too racy for their sixth or seventh grader. Actually, since the cover of the book is not always a good indication of the sexual or literary content of the interior, young

> **Fantasy is very appealing to Young Adult readers**
>
> Young adults are some of the most avid readers of fantasy. Knowing about fantasy fiction and being able to talk intelligently about the genre, even about a few authors or a few series, will win a librarian an immense amount of respect from this sometimes difficult age group. However, you cannot pretend to know what you are talking when you don't—and hope to retain their respect. So, if you work with young adults, if you work in a small public library where young adults are an integral part of those who read your adult collection, and you want to talk to them about fantasy, it behooves you to learn a little bit about the genre. Look for "YA" in the annotations in the Fantasy 101 bibliography or book reviews; it appears often.

readers might think they are checking out something racier or easier than they really are.

If you know you should read fantasy in order to be a better readers' advisor—and you really think you will hate it, it might be easier to begin with some of the YA titles. They are thinner; the print is a little bit bigger; they probably have a few more illustrations in them—all this will help.

Fantasy and science fiction

In general, fantasy readers also frequently read science fiction, particularly what is referred to as "soft" science fiction—the science fiction that isn't heavy on technology. However, there are science fiction purists who do not read fantasy and who will be rather hostile should you suggest fantasy titles to them. If you go to a bookstore where fantasy and science fiction are interfiled (and I have studied this in a variety of bookstores over the past few years), you will see people buying technological (or hard) science fiction books. You will also see people with an armload of a combination of softer science fiction and fantasy. You will seldom see people with a combination of both hard science fiction *and* fantasy. This is one of those generalizations that can help you when you first begin to talk to your patrons about fantasy fiction. If a patron is talking to you about fantasy, and you sense that you are speaking to a fantasy reader, this is probably not the patron to whom you could recommend Isaac Asimov or Robert Heinlein as another author to try.

However, readers of historical fiction might be pleasantly surprised when they try reading a fantasy. A good fantasy builds realistic worlds and fully drawn characters, so you will find that there is crossover between those who read fantasy and those who read historical fiction. Quite a bit of fantasy is grounded in Celtic lore and builds upon the theory that the coming of the Romans and Christianity suppressed the Celtic culture along with its people. The Celtic culture included the land of faerie; it included magic; it included the Druids. The Romans were much more pragmatic in their dealing with their gods. Then came the Christians, and of course, unless your magic was that of Jesus Christ and the accepted miracles of Christianity, it couldn't exist. Magic and faerie gradually withdrew from our world. Writers of fantasy suggest we are the poorer for it and seek to rekindle the magic in their writing. Bradley's *Mists of Avalon* is a good example of this point of view. Among writers of fantasy, there are quite a few with majors in history (particularly medieval history) and literature—just read the biographical blurbs on the book jackets.

Fantasy subgenres

TIME TRAVEL FANTASY: Time travel fantasy is a well-established subgenre that might also appeal to readers of historical fiction. These works usually begin in a more contemporary time period and then, by means of magic, move to a more distant, frequently well-drawn historical time period on earth or a parallel world, one where magic may or may not be integral to the culture. Time travel fantasies are less likely to be part of a series, so reading one is more likely to be a one-time effort on the part of the "testing" reader. These are fairly straight-forward stories about someone from a fairly contemporary time who either inadvertently ends up in another time or, for a personal or scientific reason, wants to end up in another time. A classic time travel title is Richard Matheson's *Bid Time Return*. The movie version, *Somewhere in Time*, with Christopher Reeve, has caused many a teenage girl to lose her heart. Interlibrary loan librarians took a while to figure out that the burgeoning interest in this book came from the teenage females who stayed through the end of the movie, read the credits and discovered the title and author of the book. It has since been republished with the title, *Somewhere in Time*, and has its own page on the Internet.

SWORD AND SORCERY: Sword and sorcery is a strong subgenre of fantasy. These are the swashbucklers of the genre—with some authors more concerned with the "sword," others with the "sorcery." All in all, it should not be surprising that there are a goodly number of fantasy writers who are practitioners of the martial arts (judo, karate), and several who are members of the Society for Creative Anachronism and who participate in their medieval reenactments. It's not just the sword and sorcery writer who benefits from an understanding of fighting technique and battle strategy. The confrontations between good and evil are integral to most fantasy—and many involve actual physical battles between the opposing forces. Someone who knows something about fighting and something about defense is going to be able to write a better battle scene than someone who doesn't. No one likes to read about a battle and not be able to figure out how a character got from here with a sword in hand to "over there" with a broken knife. Sword and sorcery that is heavier on the sword might appeal to less pragmatic readers of military historicals or to those who enjoy swashbucklers. Fritz Leiber's **Fafhrd and the Gray Mouser** is a classic sword and sorcery series—it's nicely bawdy, too.

URBAN FANTASY: Urban fantasy is a new kind of gritty fantasy that I find very intriguing. Action is set in a contemporary urban setting that can be either an actual city (like Ottawa, Canada) or an imaginary city (de Lint's Newford). Its protagonists are usually the people who live in the city and on the fringes of society (artists, students, musicians, street people, people who work in the missions). Somehow they come in contact with the remnants of the world of faerie who retreated from the upper world when humans began moving in and made life unpleasant for them. These faerie have made a home in the underground world, the train tunnels, the vacant buildings. If you enjoyed the old television series, *One Step Beyond*, you might find similarities between the atmosphere and subject of its shows and urban fantasy, especially short stories. Readers of horror fiction might find these works an engaging cross-over.

HUMOROUS FANTASY: Humorous fantasy fiction can be pretty broad. It can have the kind of yuk, yuk humor in it that young people like. It can, particularly in the fifteenth to twentieth book of the series, get a bit hard for some people to endure. Piers Anthony's **Xanth** is a series that many young people discover and pass around among themselves. **Xanth** books are sprinkled throughout with puns. Anthony is so known for his puns that readers send him their puns, and he seems to feel obligated to use these puns in newer **Xanth** tales. There is a certain time period in young people's lives when they love this stuff. If you introduce young readers to **Xanth**, their parents will never forgive you, but the readers will love you.

You will find that several fantasy authors have strong music backgrounds and that music frequently plays a key role in both the life of the protagonists and the magic of the tale. If you think about it, this is really pretty logical. Magic involves spells and incantations, where the rhythms of music would be helpful. An underlying thread in much fantasy is the belief in the magic of words—that old songs, prayers and poems are keys to forgotten knowledge (de Lint, Lackey).

Coming up with the right nursery rhyme each time

The hero in Christopher Stasheff's **Warlock** series has to recite an appropriate nursery rhyme to generate the necessary magic to get himself out of trouble. While he is fighting off monsters or whatever else he might be doing, he's trying to think, "Now what nursery rhyme is going to stick a sword in my hand? What nursery rhyme is going to turn my enemy into a pile of goo so I don't have to worry about it?" Readers enjoy the way the books are printed because the character's predicament is at the bottom of the page, and it's not until you turn the page that you figure out what nursery rhyme our hero has remembered just in time to rescue himself. It's a bit of a reader's challenge to see if you can come up with the right rhyme—which is something that has a great appeal to his readers. There is another Stasheff series where the hero's magic spells have to be in four-line rhymes. I have a junior-high-aged nephew who has been driving his mother crazy since reading one of these books. He can't ask for a glass of water without tossing off a four-line bit of doggerel…

The series phenomenon

You have probably noticed how much fantasy is published as trilogies, quartets, and more. When you read selection journals and you see a series that has 80 million titles, you think about your shelf space and you ask yourself, "Why, oh why, do these authors keep on writing series after series?" Well, when the author has gone to all the trouble to build a civilization and populate it with fully realized, believable characters, it would be a terrible shame to waste it on one 300-page visit. You will also find that readers (and sometimes authors) just can't allow a world or character die. An author will write a book that is very popular and ten years later, fifteen years later, a sequel will appear simply because the author has finally been convinced to write another episode by the fans (or editors) who wanted to know what happened next—or what happened before. It was nearly twenty years between Dickson's *Dragon and the George* and the now nearly annual further adventures of the **Dragon Knight**, a poor grad student who participated in a time travel experiment. He not only ended up in the past, but he became a dragon—which was slightly inconvenient (even for a psychology major). When you read the first novel now, the scientific explanation of the 1970s-vintage time machine and the depiction of campus life are showing their age, but the basic story is still quite engaging. Some authors have been in certain worlds so long that they are facing burnout, which might be why more and more shared authorship of titles is coming into play. This is particularly horrendous for catalogers, who want to classify by author, and for readers, who want all of a series to be in the same place (see the **Trillium Series** in the bibliography).

Fantasy fiction and the bookstore

In the face of budget realities and space limitations, librarians need to be able to gauge patron interest in a genre. At a local superstore in Bloomington, Illinois, the store wrapped its Fantasy/Science Fiction section around the aisle to add another range of shelves less than a year after its opening. What's waiting to be shelved boggles the mind—until you come back two days later and, not only is nothing left to be shelved, but there are "spaces" on the shelves. Another bookstore in Bloomington has added at least two full sections of fantasy and science fiction in the last two years—at the expense of two sections of mystery. (It might be worth noting that the store cut back on mystery, not romance or westerns.) This store also has a new section near the front cash register for the fantasy role playing and gaming books, which used to be back with the rest of the science fiction and fantasy books. The location is probably for security purposes much like the way a library keeps certain books close to the circulation desk. The store also has several end displays of fantasy that change on a regular basis. Bookstores wouldn't be making these changes if they didn't have the necessary customer base.

If bookstores are doing such a good business selling fantasy, and fantasy readers seem to buy so much, why should a library "waste" precious shelf space for the stuff? Well, if your library has selected popular materials center as one of its roles, then fantasy is part of the popular materials collection. Fantasy readers, like everyone else, can't afford to buy everything they like. Even if a fantasy reader wants to own all of a certain series, he/she won't know from day one that a series is one to read from beginning to end, much less a series to own. The library is the ideal place for fantasy readers to discover or sample a new or new-to-them author. By sampling a series in your library, by being able to read the first book in a series or other titles by that author, the patron can decide whether this is something to purchase—or if this is one of those authors or series to borrow from the library. Most fantasy readers have limited shelf space in their homes.

A library has just so much shelf space, too. It is not possible for most libraries to stock all of the fantasy published—not even just the "good" fantasy. There's just too much of it. Even if most fantasy is still published in paperback and is not too tall and sometimes not too fat, library shelves do tend to fill up. What's a library to do? First, pay attention to what your patrons ask for and what they request on interlibrary loan, then buy in those areas. If you haven't spent money on fantasy in the past, it's not a bad idea to track interlibrary loan requests and to talk to your patrons who read the fantasy you now have. Build your collection around the primary needs of your community.

Talk to your patrons who read the fantasy you now have and see what other titles or authors they would like to read.

Fantasy and cooperative collection management

Because there are series that have lots of volumes and there are lots of series, fantasy is an area that is a good candidate for cooperative collection management. If you have the first book in the series and have agreements with other libraries about who is to carry all titles in a certain series, you can rely on your shared database and interlibrary loan to meet patron demand. A fantasy reader generally doesn't mind waiting. They won't wait forever but, when one is used to waiting for sequels that take several years to appear, what is several weeks? The key is to have titles visible on your regional database. Then the patron knows there is a good chance the items she wants to read are somewhere fairly close by.

You might want to surf your regional database and check it against fantasy bibliographies like those listed in the readers' advisory bibliography at the end of this handbook to see which libraries have fantasy collections similar to yours—or larger, stronger fantasy collections. See what authors are in other libraries that might be authors your patrons are interested in. Get together for tea, coffee, whatever and talk with your fellow librarians. See if you can come up with some sort of agreement on fantasy cooperative collection management.

Don't limit developing cooperative ventures to the purchase of new titles, also think about retention plans and last copy centers. You might still have to buy every **Xanth** book that comes out to meet the immediate demand of your patrons who read the series. But, after a year or two, if you are in a cooperative, you might not need to keep them all. You might need to retain the first one or two, and the most recent titles, but you can use the cooperative to meet the needs of patrons new to the series. Small libraries might want to keep certain classic authors, certain titles that circulate constantly and titles that show up on local school reading lists. After you build a basic collection, other titles you choose to retain will differ according to your patrons' reading interests.

If you track how your collection is used and what you borrow from other libraries, you will find that you are retooling your fantasy collection on a fairly regular basis. Reading tastes change. Although many authors are going to be around for a long time, others are like cotton candy—the first "taste" was wonderful, but the substance just isn't there. Generally, when a second title is downhill and the third is awful, most fantasy readers give up on an author or series. So, the more frequently you pay attention to what's going on in your own collection, the quicker you can weed the cotton candy titles, and the better use you can make of valuable shelf space.

Readers' advisory services

To provide good readers' advisory service in fantasy, you have to read in the genre, and you have to read across the genre. You do have to take the medicine.

    If you absolutely cannot commit to reading in a genre, then the best thing you can do for your patrons is to purchase genre guides like those on the readers' advisory resources list at the end of this handbook, leave them in full view and let your patrons make their own decisions. But, if you are going to be a true readers' advisor to your patrons in fantasy or any other genre, you have to have read enough of the genre yourself so that you can communicate effectively with its readers. Fantasy readers are so appreciative of librarians with even the most basic understanding of the genre. They will respect your efforts, and they are generally quite willing to tell you what they think is good, what's not good, what's different. Talk to your patrons and take a lead from what they are saying. Share bibliographies with them and see what they say about them—where they agree, where they disagree. It will help you get a better feeling for what they like, what they don't like.

    To help you get started reading in the fantasy genre, two short bibliographies follow this section. The first is a list of classics titled Fantasy You Should Try to Read: Fantasy 101. If that is too daunting, try the next bibliography, You Should Read Some Fantasy, But You Still Don't Want To... which recommends titles that might be palatable to readers of other genres such as romance and mystery.

Use your patrons to help you build your expertise and background knowledge—particularly if you are building a fantasy collection from scratch.

Fantasy you should try to read: Fantasy 101

If you read everything on this list, you will have put your big toe in and swirled it around the pool of nearly every subgenre of fantasy. The list was compiled from various sources and the suggestions of many fantasy readers (several of them librarians—all of them quite opinionated). When it comes to building a basic collection for a library, these would certainly be good titles to include. If you serve young people who are required to read in different genres, this would not be a bad list of books to have on hand. You will notice that some of the titles are generally considered to be children's or young adult books. They are still classics in the field of fantasy.

Alexander, Lloyd. **Chronicles of Prydain:** *The Book of Three.* New York: Holt, 1964.

> A contemporary classic of heroic fantasy for both older children and YA's. This is the story of an Assistant Pig-Keeper who becomes a king, and a magical princess who gives up her magic to become his queen. They battle good and evil and save their world as they grow up.

Anthony, Piers. **Magic of Xanth series:** *A Spell for Chameleon.* New York: Del Ray, 1987.

> A light-hearted adventure series filled with witty dialogue and wordplay, set in Xanth, a medieval world where all living things have magical powers. Xanth lies adjacent to Mundania, a non-magic world shaped like Florida (home of the author). The series has a well-rounded cast of characters who dabble in magic, quests, battles, romance and a great many puns, often execrable, frequently hilarious. A series that introduces many a ten-year-old to the world of "adult" fantasy.

Beagle, Peter S. *The Last Unicorn.* New York: NAL Dutton, 1991.

> A unicorn, afraid she might be the last of her kind, sets off on a quest to find the other lost unicorns. Schmendrick, a magician, joins her and helps her. This is a classic quest novel with strong symbolism.

Bradbury, Ray, *Something Wicked This Way Comes.* New York: Knopf, 1983.

> A compelling fantasy narrative about two small boys fighting evil forces when the Dark Carnival comes to their small midwestern town. This has been made into a fine movie. The movie producers took some of the elements that were hinted at as manifestations of evil or dark in the book and created a movie that can scare the heck out of you without a lot of blood and gore.

Bradley, Marion Zimmer. *Mists of Avalon.* New York: Del Ray, 1985.

> The Arthurian legend from the point of view of Morgana, priestess of the "old ways."

Brooks, Terry. **Shannara series:** *The Sword of Shannara.* New York: Del Ray, 1983.

> Likable protagonists, imaginative plots and rich detail characterize this epic fantasy which spans several hundred years. In the Four Lands, a magical world of the future, men, dwarves and elves are entangled in a dangerous and exciting fight against dark, repressive forces. YA's love this series.

Carroll, Lewis. *Alice in Wonderland.* Chicago: Children's Press, 1969. *(Alice's Adventures in Wonderland was first published in 1866.)*

> Human from the "real world" crosses over into a fantasyland where she has many strange adventures before returning home. Yes, it's fantasy!

Cooper, Susan. **The Dark is Rising series:** *The Dark is Rising.* New York: Simon & Schuster Children's, 1973.

> Written for children and YA's, an adult will enjoy them. *The Grey King* won the Newbery Award. The books can be read on several levels—as a simple adventure or as a grand conflict between good and evil filled with allegory and symbolism.

de Lint, Charles. *Dreams Underfoot.* New York, Tor, 1994.

> Tales of contemporary and urban fantasy where those who live on the fringes of our society touch the realm of faerie. His books are stand-alones, though interrelated. His urban fantasy has a gritty reality to it that might appeal to readers of darker contemporary fiction.

Dickson, Gordon R. **Dragon Knight series:** *Dragon and the George.* New York: Del Ray, 1987.

> An American grad student participates in a time travel experiment and ends up in a parallel world similar to medieval England—in the body of a dragon. Nice humorous fantasy with well-drawn recurring characters.

Donaldson, Stephen R. **Chronicles of Thomas Covenant the Unbeliever:** *Lord Foul's Bane.* New York: Del Ray, 1987.

> The protagonist of this epic fantasy is Thomas Covenant, an alienated leper. Covenant's dream-like adventures take him to the magical world of The Land, where he is thought to be a legendary and powerful hero. Traveling back and forth between the two worlds, Covenant at times wonders if his experiences in The Land are delusions related to his disease. An introspective series in which the author carefully develops the moral stature of his hero.

Eddings, David. **The Belgariad:** *Pawn of Prophecy.* New York: Del Ray, 1986.

> Set in a barbarian world, these colorful tales are epic fantasy in the tradition of Tolkien. Men, kings and gods are embroiled in conflicts that date back to ancient times. The heroes attempt to thwart evil powers which endanger the future of the universe. Eddings' characters always manage to say the things you always wish you had said when you think back on a conversation. **The Malloreon** is a sequel; **Belgrath** is the prequel series.

Fairy Tales: A Series of Modern Fantasy Novels Retelling Classic Fairy Tales

> A variety of fantasy authors are writing new versions of traditional fairy tales for this series. The retellings incorporate myth and folklore, but the approach to each fairy tale is original. The authors have chosen both modern and historical settings for their classics. For example, Patricia Wrede sets *Snow White and Rose Red* in a magical Elizabethan England. Charles de Lint's *Jack the Giant-Killer* exists in a dark, contemporary Ottawa alongside an invisible fairy world. Pamela Dean's *Tam Lin* is set on a Minnesota college campus. Jane Yolen's *Briar Rose* is a powerful, haunting Holocaust allegory.

Feist, Raymond. **Riftwar Saga:** Includes *Magician: Apprentice.* New York: Bantam, 1986.

> Enjoyable parallel worlds saga, with the twist that both worlds have magic. This and the companion series, **Daughter of the Empire** (New York: Bantam, 1988), by Feist and Janny Wurts, have a strong romantic element. Feist's new Midkemia trilogy is **The Serpentwar Saga** (*Rise of a Merchant Prince.* New York: Morrow, 1995. *Shadow of a Dark Queen.* New York: Morrow, 1994).

Finney, Jack. *Time and Again.* New York: Simon & Schuster, 1986.

> The original, classic, time travel, romantic fantasy was recently joined by a new, good, but not-quite-as-good sequel.

Foster, Alan Dean. **Spellsinger series:** *Spellsinger.* New York: Warner Books, 1988.

> Light-hearted series which exploits all the cliches of contemporary fantasy and still manages to be fresh and original. A guitar player from our world is transferred to a magical realm, where he discovers that he is a sorcerer as long as he can play or sing. The only problem is, he has to come up with the right song for things to go as he wishes!

Gardner, John. *Grendel.* New York: Knopf, 1971.

> The story of Beowulf—from the monster's point of view. In the retelling of the Old-English epic, Grendel emerges as more human than the heroes, and they, in turn, appear more monstrous and brutish than this very sympathetic monster.

Garrett, Randall. **Lord Darcy series:** *Too Many Magicians.* Boston: Gregg Press, 1978.

> A series of murder mysteries set in an alternate England where magic works. Lord Darcy and Sherlock Holmes could be close kin.

Goldman, William. *The Princess Bride.* Mattituck, NY: Amereon Ltd., 1976.

> No introduction to fantasy is complete without this parody of fairy tales, swashbucklers and fantasy cliches.

Gregorian, Joyce Ballou. **The Tredana Trilogy:** *The Broken Citadel.* OP

> This parallel worlds story begins when an eleven-year-old girl slips into another world. Each book takes place about ten years after the previous one. This series is among the relatively few which use Middle Eastern mythology as a base, rather than Celtic or Norse myths.

Hambly, Barbara. **Darwath trilogy:** *The Time of the Dark.* New York: Del Ray, 1984.

> A series in the Tolkien mold. The fight against the evil Dark is undertaken by a wizard, Ingold Inglorian, and two young Californians, Gil and Rudy, Ingold enlists in the battle. Gil, the former history student becomes an accomplished swordswoman; Rudy, the biker/van scene painter becomes a magician. They become involved with the land and its people—not with each other.

————. **Sun Wolf series:** *The Ladies of Mandrigyn.* New York: Del Ray, 1984.

> A mercenary captain discovers he is a wizard in a world where magic is not respected. The business/romance relationship with his female second-in-command is an interesting thread throughout the series.

Jordan, Robert. **The Wheel of Time:** *The Eye of the World.* New York, Tor, 1990.

> In the mythic village of Edmond's Field, a handful of ordinary villagers are thrown into a cosmic conflict to save the world from the evil Ba'alzamon. The women's magic society, the Aes Sedai, is a bit like the Bene Gesserit of Frank Herbert's *Dune.* A heroic quest fantasy in the Tolkien vein. It's a fully created world, and the devices are new and they work. The characters are well developed. Jordan appeals to YA's today, as Terry Brooks' **Shannara** did over a decade ago. The individual volumes are huge, and the first book takes a while to get going—but then you are most likely hooked for the duration of the series.

Kurtz, Katherine. **Chronicles of the Deryni:** *Deryni Rising.* New York: Del Ray, 1987.

> Kurtz is in the process of writing her fourth trilogy set in the land of Gwynedd, a vaguely medieval, definitely Celtic fantasy world. The Deryni are practitioners of magic. They are a minority population and are subject to all the fears and prejudices of being in the minority. Good and evil humans, not gods and goddesses, vie for supremacy. Anyone who likes historical fiction and wants to get started in fantasy would probably enjoy these. Her Internet newsgroup is: alt.books.deryni.

————. *The Adept.* New York: Ace Books, 1991.

> The first title in a series of the same name. A modern Scottish psychiatrist and Master of the Old Ways works with law enforcement agencies in the solving of crimes perpetuated by modern disciples of the Dark. A nice blend of fantasy and detection.

Lackey, Mercedes. **The Last Herald-Mage:** *Magic's Pawn.* New York: DAW, 1989.

> All these take place in the same secondary world, called Valdemar. The first series is the only one written specifically for YA's. In it, a teenage girl finds her true destiny and saves the world, with the help of her Companion, a magical, sentient superhorse. Lackey is particularly good with strong female characters. Lackey's newsgroup is: alt.books.m-lackey.

Lawhead, Stephen. **The Paradise War:** *The Song of Albion.* New York: Avon, 1993.

> Two Oxford students, in Scotland for a weekend, seek and find a gateway to Celtic Britain (not Arthurian). Lawhead is one of the few contemporary writers of inspirational fantasy fiction. Be warned, his Arthurian quartet is downhill after the first two books.

LeGuin, Ursula K. **Earthsea:** *A Wizard of Earthsea.* Berkeley, Calif.: Parnassus, c1968.

> A classic of contemporary fantasy that follows the life and the light-dark conflicts faced by a mage from his impetuous youth to his wiser later years.

Leiber, Fritz. **Fafhrd and the Gray Mouser:** *Swords in the Mist.* Boston: Gregg Press, 1977.

> True, robust sword and sorcery. Recommend to readers who enjoy bawdy adventure fiction. Two barbarian adventurers crisscross their ancient world—surviving, if not winning.

Lewis, C.S. **The Chronicles of Narnia:** *The Lion, the Witch, and the Wardrobe.* New York: Macmillan, 1983.

> Lucy goes through the back of a wardrobe and finds the land of Narnia. Her brothers and sister eventually follow, and they defeat the White Witch with the help of Aslan, a lion, and become Kings and Queens of Narnia.

Many an adult fantasy reader read and enjoyed this classic quest fantasy as a child. Lewis is the dean of inspirational (Christian) fantasy fiction. Other Christian fiction authors who have written fantasy are George MacDonald and Madeline L'Engle.

MacAvoy, R.A. *Tea With the Black Dragon*. New York: Doubleday, 1983.

A gentle contemporary fantasy set in San Francisco—with a mystery thrown in. The two main characters are a middle-aged musician searching for her missing daughter, and an ageless Chinese scholar who claims to have begun life as a black dragon. The sequel is *Twisting the Rope*.

McKillip, Patricia. **Riddle of the Stars:** *The Riddle-Master of Hed*. New York: Ballantine, 1985.

A good quest fantasy and story of enduring love and devotion often found in the YA section.

McKinley, Robin. *The Blue Sword* (New York: Greenwillow, 1982) and *The Hero and the Crown* (New York: Greenwillow, 1984)

These two good quest fantasies are set in a mythical land of Damar with a Middle Eastern flavor. The books are interconnected by the magic sword wielded by two women warriors in different times. The heroines are strong; the romantic element is very believable. Great read-alouds; the first won the Newbery Award.

Matheson, Richard. *Bid Time Return*. New York: Viking, 1975.

The classic time travel fantasy on which the movie *Somewhere in Time* was based. A good novel for introducing fantasy to reluctant female YA's. Matheson is generally better known for his horror titles.

Norton, Andre. **Witch World:** *Witch World*. New York, Ace Books, 1986.

Popular continuing sword and sorcery series with English/Celtic overtones. Good escapist reading with strong female characters. The first twenty were all Norton; now a "shared world" saga with other writers taking up the skein. Recommended for YA's.

Pierce, Meredith Ann. **Darkangel Trilogy:** *The Darkangel*. Boston: Little, Brown, c1982.

Very evocative, atmospheric tale steeped in vampire legends and mythology with gothic and romantic elements. A very interesting examination of the vampire as a creature who is trapped into doing things simply by the nature of his being and seems to be evil incarnate. The heroine realizes that he has a glimmer of heart or soul that is redeemable—not particularly good, but redeemable. The ending will surprise most readers.

Pini, Wendy and Richard. **ElfQuest:** *Fire and Flight*. Poughkeepsie, NY: Father Tree Press, 1993.

A series of *very* fine graphic novels about the meeting and reunion of three tribes of elves, the warrior-hunter Wolfriders, the gentle agrarian Sun Folk, and the primitive Go-backs who were separated ages ago when their ancestors were attacked by early humans. The characters, their lives and culture are fully developed. Wendy Pini's art work sets a standard rarely achieved in graphic novels. Several non-graphic shared world anthologies are *not* recommended by many **ElfQuest** readers.

Rawn, Melanie. **Dragon Prince:** *Dragon Prince*. New York: DAW, 1988.

Some label these as soap-operaish escapist romps—sort of Tolkien and McCaffrey crossed with Danielle Steel. Others feel they are certainly as good as Eddings with fresh takes on magic and absorbing characters that you remember and miss spending time with after you've finished the books.

Everyone agrees that Rawn's is a fully realized world with a lot of romance, a lot of magic and a lot of politics.

Stewart, Mary. **The Life of Merlin:** *The Crystal Cave.* New York: Fawcett, 1984.

Classic, but ultimately melancholy, Arthurian fantasy told from the point of view of Merlin. This series begins with his youthful adventures in the court of his grandfather, the King of Wales, and ends with his influence in the birth of King Arthur.

Tepper, Sheri S. *Beauty.* New York: Bantam, 1992.

An eerie, haunting, dark retelling of the Sleeping Beauty story.

Tolkien, J.R.R. *The Hobbit*

The true parent of all modern quest fantasies. The legends and history of Middle-earth in a series of novels taking place in this fascinating world inhabited by both good and evil beings. Among the good is a hobbit, Frodo Baggins, who must undertake a perilous journey to return a potentially evil ring to the Mountain of Fire, where the ring was made and the only place it can be destroyed. The Hobbit introduces Middle-earth and is the easiest read by younger readers.

The Trillium Series

This is a good introduction to the "shared world" concept. *Black Trillium* (New York: Doubleday, 1990), the first in the series, was co-authored by Marion Zimmer Bradley, Julian May, and Andre Norton with each author developing and plotting the story of one of three sisters with very different personalities who must come together to save their land. Then May wrote *Blood Trillium* (New York: Bantam, 1992); Norton wrote *Golden Trillium* (New York: Bantam, 1992); Bradley wrote *Lady of the Trillium* (New York: Bantam, 1995), and Norton is writing *Sky Trillium.* There are other shared world fantasies—and all drive catalogers crazy! It's interesting to see three very fine authors take a common beginning and put their own personalities and twists on the story.

Walton, Evangeline. **The Books of the Welsh Mabinogion:** *The Prince of Annwn.* New York: Simon & Schuster, 1992.

A heavily researched, classic retelling and expansion of classic Welsh myths into a cohesive series of novels. A true blend of magic, mystery and a clash of cultures.

Weis, Margaret and Tracy Hickman. **Dragonlance Chronicles:** *Dragons of Autumn Twilight.* Lake Geneva, Wis.: TSR, c1984.

The **Chronicles** is followed by the **Legends**, which is followed by the **Tales**, which is followed by the **Heroes**.... All are set in the Dragonlance game universe created by TSR, Inc. for a series of fantasy role-playing games. YA's, particularly those into gaming, will eat these up. If you are not into fantasy gaming, avoid Dragonlance tales by other authors; they are not as good.

White, T.H. *The Once and Future King.* New York: Ace Books.

Once is the book on which the musical *Camelot* was based. The first section, "The Sword in the Stone," was also made into a Disney movie. This has become the modern standard retelling of the Arthurian legend.

Zelazny, Roger. **Amber series:** *Nine Princes of Amber.* New York: Avon, 1977.

This complex series spins threads of political intrigue, the tarot, magic, adventure, swordplay and the nature of reality. It takes place in Amber, the one true world, during the distant past. Oberon, King of Amber, disappears, leaving the nine princes to fight over the crown. The first five books chronicle the maturing of Corwin, Prince of Amber, as he tries to solve his father's disappearance, save the world from chaotic collapse, come to terms with his rather bizarre family and become king himself. The second group of books follows the adventures of Corwin's son, Merlin.

You *should* read some fantasy, but you still *don't want to.....*

This is the closest I could come to creating a "cheat sheet" for non-readers. If you know you should read fantasy and you still really truly in your heart think you don't want to, give some of these crossover or read-alike titles a try.

For bawdy fiction, try Fritz Leiber's **Fafhrd and the Gray Mouser.**

For contemporary urban fiction try Emma Bull's *War for the Oaks* (heroine is a rock musician), Charles de Lint's tales of Newford, or Elizabeth Scarborough's *Godmother* (humorous trials of a fairy godmother in contemporary Seattle).

For those who haven't outgrown fairy tales, there are several good choices. Try **Fairy Tales: A Series**, William Goldman's *The Princess Bride* (a humorous parody), Robin McKinley's *Deerskin* (good study of the psychological effects of incest on a young woman), Elizabeth Scarborough's *Godmother* (fairy godmother in contemporary Seattle), and Sherri S. Tepper's *Beauty.*

A good ghost story is Peter Beagle's *A Fine and Private Place*, written when the author was only nineteen.

Readers of Gothics should enjoy Meredith Ann Pierce's **Darkangel Trilogy.**

Readers of historical fiction have many choices. The time period is in parenthesis. Some suggestions include Peter Ackroyd's *Hawksmoor* (Seventeenth-century London), Poul Anderson's *Ys* (Roman Empire), Clare Bell's **Clan Ground** (Aztec), Marion Zimmer Bradley's *Mists of Avalon* (Arthur), Orson Scott Card's **Tales of Alvin Maker** (Nineteenth-century U.S.), John Ford's *Dragon Waiting* (Fifteenth-century Europe), Diana Gabaldon's *Outlander* (Jacobite Scotland), Jennifer Roberson's **Lady of the Forest** (Robin Hood), Mary Stewart's **Life of Merlin** (Arthur), Judith Tarr's **Hound and the Falcon** (Twelfth-century Europe), and Connie Willis' *Lincoln's Dreams.*

For fans of Hollywood and the movies, there is Craig Shaw Gardner's **Cineverse Cycle** ("B" movie world) and Barbara Hambly's *Bride of the Rat God* (1920s Hollywood).

Readers of horror fiction can try Meredith Ann Pierce's **Darkangel Trilogy** and Tim Powers' *Anubis Gates.*

Fans of humorous fiction might like Piers Anthony's **Xanth**, Robert Lynn Asprin's **Myth Series**, Gordon R. Dickson's **Dragon Knight**, Ru Emerson's **Tales of Nedao**, Alan Dean Foster's **Spellsinger**, Tom Holt's *Expecting Someone Taller* and Christopher Stasheff's **Warlock.**

Readers of inspirational fiction might try Stephen Lawhead's **Paradise War**, C. S. Lewis, and Madeline L'Engle.

For those who like literature/mythology, there are several possibilities including John Gardner's *Grendel* (Beowulf), Tom Holt (Germanic myths and legends), Guy Gavriel Kay's **Finovar** (Arthurian), Patricia Kenneally's **Keltiad** (Celts & Arthur), Diana L. Paxson's *Brisingamen* (Norse) and *The Wolf and the Raven* (Germanic), Mickey Zucker Reichert's **Bilfrost Guardians** (Norse), Evangeline Walton's **Welsh Mabinogion**, T. H. White's *Mistress Masham's Repose* (Swift's Gulliver), and Tad Williams' *Caliban's Hour* (Shakespeare's *Tempest*).

For military fiction try Chris Bunch and Allan Cole, Glen Cook's **Black Company**, Brian Daley's **Coramonde**, Elizabeth Moon's **Paksenarrion**, and Jennifer Roberson's **Tiger and Del**.

Readers of mystery and intrigue can take a look at Emma Bull's *Finder*, Glen Cook's **Garrett, P.I.**, Randall Garrett's **Lord Darcy**, Katherine Kurtz's and Deborah Turner Harris' **Adept**, R. A. MacAvoy's **Black Dragon**, L. A. Taylor's *Cat's Paw*, and Patricia Wrede's *Mairelon the Magician*.

Political fiction readers might like Feist's and Wurts' **Daughter of the Empire**, Melanie Rawn, Jennifer Roberson's **Cheysuli**, and Roger Zelazny's **Amber**.

If you like romance fiction try Clare Bell's **Clan Ground**, Teresa Edgerton's **Green Lion Trilogy**, Raymond Feist's **Riftwar**, Diana Gabaldon, Richard Matheson's *Time and Again*, Melanie Rawn's two **Dragon** trilogies, Jennifer Roberson's **Cheysuli**, and David William's *Second Sight* (movie version was called *The Two Worlds of Jennie Logan*).

Readers of thrillers might like Peter Ackroyd's *Hawksmoor*.

If you are intrigued by the idea of time travel (from now to then), there are many authors to look at, including Jack Finney, Diana Gabaldon, Richard Matheson, Marlys Millhiser, Tim Powers, David Williams and Connie Willis.

For Men Only
Readers' Advisory Service for Men

Chapter Seven

Introduction

Debbie Walsh

The genre sections in this chapter have been contributed by members of a Special Interest Group for Readers' Advisors which meets with the support of the DuPage Library System. The group formed in 1992 as a way for library staffers providing readers' advisory service to come together to discuss issues and share ideas, since in many libraries, readers' advising is not a separate function, or might be done by only one or two people in the building.

Each meeting of the special interest group stood alone and was rather free-ranging, depending upon who showed up and what topics they wanted to discuss. The ideas and bibliographies in this chapter grew out of a discussion of "problem patrons." We defined "problem" as an unsatisfactory exchange with a patron who wanted a recommendation, or a follow-up exchange with a patron who was dissatisfied with a recommendation. The pattern that emerged as we went around the table (a table at which there was only one male librarian seated) was that male patrons posed our most serious challenges. We were very unsure of what they would read and, perhaps even more telling, of what they would *not* read. We were also, as a result, very uneasy about approaching them and offering help.

We began to relate *successful* encounters with male patrons, and by the time the meeting was winding down, we had come up with some genres and types of books which seemed to work with a greater degree of success than others. The time allotted for the meeting came to an end, and the group was still brainstorming—so it was quickly decided that this was a topic which we could discuss fruitfully for several meetings.

Since the group met every other month, we agreed on six categories of works of fiction we *thought* men would read, and plotted the next six meetings on our calendars, assigning a category per meeting. Four of these six categories will be addressed in this chapter. We all committed to reading several books thought to be representative of the category as "homework" and to trying to identify characteristics and appeal—common elements the books might share. We decided that if nothing else came of these meetings, at least we would gain confidence in talking about a number of books we might not have read ourselves, get comfortable with a few specific ones, and take away a list which we could fall back on when asked for a recommendation by a patron (male or female) who wanted a genre book. In the final analysis we determined that science fiction, general (non-genre) fiction, westerns, spy thrillers, mystery, and adventure fiction were most likely to be successfully recommended to our male readers.

We did not intend to become experts on male patrons, or readers' advising, and in retrospect, I can safely say that we probably have more questions about the nature of appeal *now* than when we started our study.

Science Fiction

Karen Kaufmann Migaldi

The discussion of science fiction was approached with no small amount of hesitation. We had only one person in our group who admitted to liking science fiction, much less reading it on a regular basis. However, we agreed to selflessly set aside our own feelings because we recognized that science fiction attracts men both as readers and as writers. Therefore, we could not adequately address the needs of our male patrons if we did not read and discuss it, hopefully discovering some common elements which make this genre appealing to them.

With one exception, we agreed to read "hard" science fiction. At this point, it might be helpful if we define "hard" science fiction. There is such a plethora of subgenres in science fiction that few experts are willing to attempt to define it. However, there is one brave individual who furnishes what he terms a "working" definition of science fiction. David Pringle, in his book entitled *Science Fiction: 100 Best Novels,* states that "science fiction is a form of fantastic fiction which exploits the imaginative perspectives of modern science."[1] This definition most closely coincides with the type of novels we chose to discuss.

A note of caution: we did not use a scientific method to compile our information. Since many of us do not regularly read science fiction, we approached our assignment in many different ways. This process ranged from merely selecting a title from our science fiction collections to choosing a title from a reference source or to relying on a patron's recommendation. We were interested in a wide range of titles, hoping that our comparison would give us a fuller idea of this genre and therefore, the type of fiction that men read. When you use the bibliographies, keep in mind that these titles will not necessarily appeal to every reader.

Returning briefly to our exception, he was our one admitted fan of science fiction. Since he regularly reads science fiction, claiming to enjoy little else, we asked him to select a fantasy title. By contrasting fantasy with science fiction, we hoped to find elements in science fiction which make it particularly appealing to men. Our efforts produced a lively discussion. Most participants agreed that they were pleasantly surprised; they actually liked science fiction.

Our diehard science fiction fan, though, did not fare so well. While he admitted that he enjoyed his title, *The Dragon and the George* by Gordon Dickson, he found it rather "fluffy." He was not satisfied with it and therefore, would probably not read more fantasy. He believed that most male patrons seek more substance in their science fiction. They want some sense of reality or plausibility. In his opinion, this title was geared towards young adults.

In our discussion, we did find several elements which stood out in the science fiction titles we read. Throughout the most successful science fiction novels, ele-

We intentionally ignored fantasy and many of the newer permutations of science fiction, believing that these forms attract more women and young adults than men. In our experience, it is "hard" science fiction which attracts men.

ments follow a logical progression. These elements include but are not limited to plot, characters and the known scientific universe. Whether it is the time travel of Philip Dick's *Now Wait for Last Year* or the computer-driven world of Orson Scott Card's *Ender's Game*, events unfold in a logical sequence. Readers do not appreciate loose ends or convenient explanations. Characters must remain true to original descriptions the author has presented. They should not act out of character unless the author provides some explanation. Finally, science of the future should be based on science of the present. If it cannot be done in today's world, then the author had better provide a good explanation of how future humanity accomplishes it.

Many science fiction novels also emphasize plot over relationships. We surmised that exploring relationships could bog down the story. Above all, our patrons seek fast-paced novels. Pacing also explains the presence of adventure in science fiction. As in the *Wheel of Time* series by Robert Jordan, it moves the plot. Adventure may be fostered by war or by cataclysmic events, but ultimately, the protagonist encounters a wide variety of situations which test his/her skills, wrenching the reader from his own mundane existence.

Science fiction actually began when Jules Verne started to explore the effects of science and technology on humanity. Therefore, actual science has always played a fundamental role. In fact, readers of hard science fiction are attracted to writers like Frederick Pohl and Isaac Asimov precisely because their novels are rooted in real science.

It is perhaps a contradiction to seek realism in general fiction much less in science fiction, a genre known for its fantastic conceptualizations, but this element ultimately defines all the others. Readers want to explore possibilities and different outcomes. However, if these potential futures seem implausible, the readers of hard science fiction will be dissatisfied and often refuse to finish the book.

Notes
1. Pringle, David. *Science Fiction: 100 Best Novels*. New York: Carroll & Graf, 1985. p. 9.

Science fiction bibliography

Anthony, Piers. Magic of Xanth series. 1977.

> A parallel world series, where a scientific world and a fantasy world interface. People cross between the worlds and each has different "talents."

Bear, Greg. *The Forge of God*. New York: Tor, 1987.

> Americans in several walks of life face the destruction of the planet brought on by mechanical agents of an alien enemy. In the sequel, *Anvil of Stars* (1992), the son of survivors takes revenge.

Bradley, Marrion Zimmer. *The Heirs of Hammerfell*. New York: DAW, 1989.

> Twin boys, the only survivors of their line, seek to restore to their father and to Hammerfell rule.

Coney, Michael. *Celestial*.

> The first book in the Song of Earth trilogy, this logical book examines parallel realities and unrealities, with characters always thinking they are somewhere else.

Dickson, Gordon. *The Dragon and the George*. New York: Del Rey, 1976.

> Jim Eckert finds himself transported to a magical Medieval England into the body of a dragon.

Other authors' series which were discussed included those by Orson Scott Card, Dan Simmons, Margaret Weiss, Robert Jordan, Greg Bear, and Jim Aiken, and the Star Wars series.

Hubbard, Ron. *Final Blackout.* Los Angeles: Bridge Publications, 1988.

> Originally published in 1940, the story takes place at the end of the world, after the Holocaust. It is the tale of a band of soldiers who have survived the bloodshed, plagues and starvation of 30 years at war.

Jordan, Robert. *The Eye of the World.* New York: T. Dorherty Assoc., 1990.

> The first volume in the Wheel of Time series, a Tolkien-like saga of a young man and his friends as they seek to defeat the forces of evil which threaten their world.

Pohl, Frederick. *World at the End of Time.* New York: Ballantine, 1990.

> A powerful, intelligent super-being wreaks havoc unintentionally on mankind.

Star Trek series. Various authors. New York: Pocket Books.

> Some are better written than others, but most appeal to people who follow the "original" and/or "new generation" TV shows and movies.

Tepper, Sheri S. *Grass.* New York: Doubleday, c1989.

> There is a plague spreading among the stars, a deadly infection that threatens to destroy all human life. It is everywhere but on "Grass," an idyllic, untouched world, covered by every type and color of grass. On Grass, humans set up their own society, based on what they knew on Earth. The truths about Grass are discovered by a new arrival, Lady Westriding.

General Fiction

Karen Kaufmann Migaldi

Unlike our experience with science fiction, we could not find precise elements which are always present in general fiction titles that appeal to men. Each book must be evaluated separately to determine if a particular patron will enjoy it. Therefore, general fiction presents the most challenging aspect of readers' advisory for men. Our discussion of this topic produced much more controversy. Some participants did not agree with all of the samples. However, in this instance, we included the titles on our list because we knew men read and enjoyed them.

The controversy that we encountered in this discussion indicates the importance of the readers' advisory interview to determine a patron's interests. While it is true that some men will only read a particular genre or type of book, the interviewer must not stereotype a reader.

One of our favorite patrons provides a good example. If you ask him who wrote the last satisfying book he read, he would probably answer Tom Clancy or W.E.B. Griffin. But, as with any avid fan, he has already read all of their books, so you can't refer him to others by these authors. However, as we soon learned, you would do him a disservice to automatically refer him to similar authors such as Stephen Coonts or Dale Brown. One day, he saw one of our staff reading *Fried Green Tomatoes at the Whistle Stop Cafe* by Fannie Flagg and requested a copy for himself. When we encountered him later, he said that he liked the book, but we should have told him about the sad scenes. It seems he was reading it on a plane and was uncomfortable reading the emotional passages in public. If we had followed our instinct with him, we would not have given him this book, and he would have missed an enriching experience.

The readers' advisory interview is an ongoing process, a technique which develops and improves with each encounter. A well-written book will stand on its own, attracting many different readers for many different reasons.

Some of the titles we discussed, such as *The Oldest Living Confederate Widow Tells All* by Allan Gurganus, appeal to men because of their strong characters. As in *The Oldest Living Confederate Widow...* or *Fried Green Tomatoes at the Whistle Stop Cafe*, the central characters are not necessarily men. *The Hotel Pastis* by Peter Mayle focuses on the central character's mid-life crisis, an issue everyone encounters on some level. Other books may appeal to men because they inform (*The Playmaker* by Thomas Keneally) or because they explore the classic theme of man against nature (*Brazil* by John Updike).

Two titles in particular evoked controversy. Many participants rejected *Before and After* by Rosellen Brown, believing that books which delve into emotions do not appeal to men. Conversely, a number of participants thought this title a good choice because it showed one man's resolution to a complex problem. And returning briefly to our patron, he enjoyed *Fried Green Tomatoes* despite the emotional passages; he just wanted some warning. Because Maeve Binchy often writes books which appeal to women, some participants thought *The Copper Beech* an inappropriate selection. Other members of our group, though, believed her titles would interest men because they focus on life in Ireland, potentially appealing to men who have visited Ireland or would like to travel there.

The variety of books which we discussed indicates the wide choice of material available to all readers. Our success as readers' advisors relies upon our ability to sift through these choices and give our patrons a truly enjoyable book. This process is an imprecise science, which we must constantly hone and perfect. We hope that our efforts offer a starting point to help you find titles that your male patrons will enjoy.

General or cross-over fiction bibliography

Archer, Jeffrey. *Honor Among Thieves*. New York: HarperCollins, 1993.

> Saddam Hussein, in league with the Mafia, infamous forgers and a special assistant to President Clinton, plots to steal and destroy the Declaration of Independence. An American professor and his lover, a Mossah agent, help the CIA to thwart the evil plan.

Binchy, Maeve. *The Copper Beech*. New York: Delacorte, 1992.

> Examines a generation in the lives of the residents of an Irish village, as seen from each character's perspective.

Brown, Rosellen. *Before and After*. New York: Farrar Straus Giroux, 1992.

> When a teenage son becomes a suspect in a brutal murder, other family members have strong but varying reactions.

Gurganus, Allan. *Oldest Living Confederate Widow Tells All*. New York: Knopf, 1989.

> Lucy Marsden regales her readers with the bittersweet story of her life. Once you've heard about Lucy's life married to a Confederate veteran, the U.S. Civil War will never be the same.

Hoeg, Peter. *Smilla's Sense of Show*. New York: Farrar Straus Giroux, 1993.

> Smilla Jaspersen, a part Inuit from Greenland, is an expert on ice and snow. When her young friend, Isaiah, suddenly dies, she is determined to find his killer. Very soon her own life is in danger as she follows the clues in this complex case.

Hoffman, Alice. *At Risk*. New York: Putnam, 1988.

> The impact of AIDS on an 11-year-old girl, her family, friends and town, as they struggle to face reality, challenges the reader to examine his own preconceptions.

Kemprecos, Paul. *Death in Deep Water.* New York: Doubleday, 1992.

"Soc," a private investigator, is hired to prove that a suspect is innocent of murder. The suspect is a killer whale at a marine park. A chance to learn about whales and dolphins while enjoying a good mystery read.

Kennally, Thomas. *The Playmaker.* New York: Simon & Schuster, 1993.

An officer at Australia's earliest penal colony casts and directs a play using inmates as actors. Based on an actual event during the 1780s.

Mayle, Peter. *Hotel Pastis: A Novel of Provence.* New York: Knopf, 1993.

A burned-out ad agency executive in midlife crisis acquires a new hotel, new scenery and a new way of life in this light, funny novel.

McCarthy, Cormac. *All the Pretty Horses.* New York: Knopf, 1992.

A coming of age story set in the modern (post 1945) West, with great sense of place and lots of male bonding.

Updike, John. *Brazil.* New York: Knopf, 1994.

Survival of a relationship and survival against the ravages of men and nature move the story in this contemporary novel.

Westerns

Sally Schuster

According to Betty Rosenberg in *Genreflecting: A Guide to Reading Interests in Genre Fiction*, "the reading of genre fiction is an escape into fantasizing."[1] The reader, for our purposes today, is a man who identifies with the hero and shares an adventure. Genre fiction is entertainment. It follows a pattern. Rules govern the plot and characters. Taboos are recognized.

Authors writing genre fiction are prolific. Often they write series, which provide the dual appeal of the author himself and the main character. We have all seen the rush to order the latest John Grisham or Lawrence Sanders novel with little regard for the reviews.

From our discussion during the For Men Only series, the participants recognized that men are more likely to read male authors, leaving the female authors for their wives or sweethearts. Men choose their books from newspaper and radio reviews, while women rely on television talk shows and word of mouth.

Some genres certainly seem to have more appeal for men. The western genre is one of those. When we think of a western, we imagine that a "lone rider is crossing the valley or desert and a shot knocks off his hat or hits a rock, startling his horse, and the range war begins."[2]

In reality, the themes and quality of writing are as varied as the writers themselves. The plot lines range from the very simple construction of Louis L'Amour's Hopalong Cassidy series to the complex action of Cormac McCarthy's *All the Pretty Horses.* While most westerns are plot-driven, some have complicated and highly developed characters.

Westerns can range in time from the early development of this country to more contemporary settings. The setting, a composite of history and scenery, is the most important element of the western.[3] Settings, which we usually think of as west of the Mississippi, can include the Ohio River Valley of some Zane Grey novels, the eastern Cherokee nation of Robert J. Conley's westerns, and even Australia.

Western heroes include cowboys, ranchers, miners, Native Americans, mountain men, border men, and more. They are skilled, independent, self-sufficient *men*, who may occasionally get involved in a little romance, but nothing that will interfere with the action.

The authors who appeal to men are mostly male. The novels are plot-oriented; they have lots of action. The conflict may be another man, or it can be nature itself. The books tend to be short. The chapters are short, and there is lots of dialog. Each story contains the lure of the frontier with its simpler times and its escape from the reality of today.

Betty Rosenberg capably summarizes the western in *Genreflecting* as "a good story, strong on adventure and thrilling action, having readily defined characters, supplying a satisfying resolution of conflicts in terms of simple blacks and whites (good and evil, right and wrong—the black and white Stetson hats of hero and villain)...."[4]

Notes

1. Betty Rosenberg. *Genreflecting: A Guide to Reading Interests in Genre Fiction.* Englewood, CO: Libraries Unlimited, 1991. p.xv.
2. Ibid., p. 17.
3. Ibid., p. 15.
4. Ibid., p. 16.

Western bibliography

Brand, Max. Any books.

Eidson, Tom. *St. Agnes' Stand.* New York: Putnam, 1994.

    A man on the run in the New Mexico Territory comes across three nuns and seven children surrounded by Apaches. Good physical descriptions.

Faust, Frederick. Any books.

Haycox, Ernest. *Head of the Mountain.* New York: New American Library, 1978, c1951.

    His gold shipments have been hijacked; he is being shot at; and someone wants his gal. Will stagecoach rider Hugh Rawson be able to settle the matters of his business and heart? Also by Haycox and recommended: *Earthbreakers* (Bridgewaters: Windsor, 1993, c1952).

Jones, Douglas C. *Season of Yellow Leaf.* New York: Holt, 1983.

    A young, white girl is captured by Comanches, raised as an Indian, and suffers with the tribe at the hands of white settlers. A sympathetic story of the clash of two cultures.

L'Amour, Louis. *Flint.* New York: Bantam, 1991.

    Flint, a man comfortable in the drawing room or in the rugged West, seeks to leave civilization behind. However, his sense of justice forces him to reveal his identity to safeguard a friend. Also by L'Amour and recommended: *Hondo* (New York: Bantam, 1983, c1953).

Matheson, Richard. *The Gun Fight.* New York: M. Evans & Co., 1993.

    A man's gotta do what a man's gotta do. Sometimes a man has no control over events and has to follow his fate (or does he?). In this novel, malicious destructive gossip pits two men against each other in a fight to the finish.

Vliet, R.G. *Solitudes.* Fort Worth: Harcourt Brace Jovanovich, 1977.

    A psychological exploration of one man's obsession.

Stories of Spies and Intrigue

Sally Schuster

As we move from the western to the spy and intrigue genre, we've traded our horse for a racy sports car. Spy and intrigue novels are a subgenre of the suspense category. John LeCarre, Robert Ludlum, and Graham Greene were not the earliest writers of the genre, but they are the ones who made it popular.

The cold war was great fodder for the genre writer. With the elimination of the Iron Curtain, authors have had to search for new settings for their novels. The Middle East and World War II are two areas being used. Terrorists, drug lords, and street gangs have replaced the Communists as the villains.

Tom Clancy increased the emphasis on technology, which has intrigued many readers. However, because of this new emphasis and the changes which are constantly occurring in world politics, these books seem to have a short shelf life. Perhaps more male-oriented book displays could provide ways to highlight older spy and intrigue titles. Displays also cater to the need for quick selection, which seems to be a characteristic of the male reader.

There are several common factors or characteristics in spy and intrigue titles which appeal to men. The story is fast-paced with lots of action, usually physical in nature. The main character is strong, well-defined, and usually male; if female, she possesses "male" personality traits. There is an emphasis on detailed, technically and/or historically accurate descriptions or settings. The good guys and bad guys are well-defined. There is not a lot of emphasis on emotions; however, strong friendships between male characters are often depicted. Intimate relationships are not a major element in these books. Sex, when present, can represent issues of control or, in the case of James Bond-type heroes, fantasy. Descriptions of these sexual encounters may be explicit, but they are not romantic. The chapters are short with lots of dialogue. There are many plot twists.

As with westerns, the level of writing varies greatly, and the amount of plot versus character ranges from the simple to the complex. As an example of the latter type, *Smilla's Sense of Snow* by Peter Hoeg is one of the more introspective spy books currently available.

The appeal of genre fiction for the reader is the sense of comfort that comes with knowing what to expect. Surprise within the boundaries of the genre is acceptable, but the book should fall within the definition of the genre to be truly satisfying. The librarian's knowledge of the authors writing in a specific genre will encourage men to ask for assistance. After all, the reader who wants the newest John LeCarre novel may not be happy if he's handed a Louis L'Amour instead.

Terrorists, drug lords, and street gangs have replaced the Communists as the villains now that the cold war era has ended.

Stories of spies and intrigue bibliography

Allbeury, Ted. *Deep Purple.* New York: Mysterious Press, c1989.

> Eddie Hoggart, an orphan, went from the Army to Intelligence to M16. Fluent in Russian, his job now is to debrief a defector named Yakunin. Yakunin finally tells of a highly placed traitor in M16 but won't give out his name. Spies, double agents, KGB, SIS, CIA, NSA, and GCHQ all come together for a great read.

Bond, Larry. *Vortex.* New York: Warner Books, 1991.

> Set in contemporary South Africa and offering a spectacle of modern weaponry, this is a book for military action lovers. A small conflict that starts at the Namibian border will soon spread to a full-scale operation. Pretty soon,

the world is faced with the nightmare of an international race war and global economic collapse.

Buckley, William F. *Saving the Queen*. New York: Doubleday, 1976.

This title is the first in a series which comes patron recommended. According to one source, they should be read in order. In this novel, Blackford Oakes begins working for the CIA. After his training, Oakes is assigned to England to help determine who is leaking information to the Soviet Union. During the course of his assignment, the Queen of England befriends him. Eventually, Oakes must choose between himself and his country.

————. *Who's On First*. New York: Avon, c1980.

Murder, torture, sex, Soviet defection, kidnapping, treachery, and good old CIA agent Blackford Oakes in a race with the Russians to be the first to put a satellite in orbit.

Cussler, Clive. *Sahara*. New York: Simon & Schuster, c1992.

Dirk Pitt is an outrageous adventurer. In *Sahara*, he discovers a Confederate ironclad, a lost plane (from 1931), and prevents a world environmental catastrophe. Packed with adventure and intrigue, Cussler's books also include interesting facts and historical tidbits. Other suggested titles: *Night Probe, Treasure*.

Deighton, Len. *Violent Ward*. New York: HarperCollins, 1993.

An abrasive, tightwad lawyer becomes embroiled in some shady deals with fellow lawyers and clients when he finds himself low on cash. He sells his practice to an entrepreneur, who happens to be married to his old childhood sweetheart, and ends up a murder suspect. Set during the Rodney King trials in chaotic Los Angeles.

Diehl, William. *27*. New York: Ballantine, c1990.

Intense action, fictional characters among historical figures, and Hitler's Germany come to life in a spy thriller that is riveting from beginning to end.

Forsyth, Frederick. *The Negotiator*. New York: Bantam, c1989.

A novel of suspense and international intrigue. Includes a cast of characters from America, Britain, Russia and Europe. A plot is devised to bring down the President of the United States in order to prevent the signing of a disarmament treaty. A real page-turner.

————. *The Odessa File*. New York: Viking, 1972.

A gripping story, much of it true, set in Germany in 1963–64, exposes the secret organization, Odessa, whose aim was to infiltrate former SS men back into the fabric of German society and into positions of power. Young journalist Peter Miller is given the diary of a survivor of the Riga Concentration Camp, run by Edward Roschmann, The Butcher of Riga. He becomes determined, for reasons of his own, to bring Roschmann to justice. An Israeli group helps Miller, but it turns into a race against time as Odessa is just as determined to hunt down and silence Miller, with Roschmann involved as a crucial player in a current plan to destroy Israel. Other suggested titles: *The Day of the Jackal, The Fourth Protocol*.

Frayn, Michael. *A Landing on the Sun*. New York: Viking Penguin, 1991.

Suspicious deaths and investigation into a 15-year-old "suicide" in the British Civil Service uncover a long-hidden scientific project of the British Government.

Gardner, John. *License Renewed*. (*James Bond in License Renewed*). New York: Charter Books, c1981, 1987.

James Bond (Agent 007) takes on the laird of a Scottish castle, a satanic master of destruction, with new gadgets and lots of skill as he saves the world from nuclear doom.

————. *Maestro.* New York: Penzler Books. 1993.

Big Herbie Kruger, retired British SIS agent and classical music enthusiast, is recalled to assist with the interrogation of an accused Nazi spy and KGB collaborator. Louis Passau, age 90, is one of the world's greatest conductors —and now, an accused spy. After an assassination attempt, the two go into hiding. There, Big Herbie skillfully draws out the Maestro's life story. Tension builds in the present as Passau reveals the past.

Granger, Bill. *The British Cross.* New York: Crown, 1983.

November Man Devereaux is sent to Helsinki to make contact with a would-be Russian defector. To clinch his case, the Russian says he can bring Tomas Crohan out from the Gulag. The mere mention of this man's name sends off alarms in the CIA, the British Secret Service, and the KGB. But the reasons remain murky; the players, devious and deadly serious. Devereaux finally unwinds the complicated strands of the whole dirty business, adds justice to the mix, and forces his own solution to the dilemma.

————. *League of Terror.* New York: Warner Books, 1992.

The eleventh book in the November Man series. Deveraux, the spy they call November, finds himself locked in a deadly battle. The backdrop is a secret war of terrorism waged by a mastermind, who combines tactics of Irish republicanism with the sleek financial machinations of Wall Street.

Hagberg, David. *Desert Fire.* New York: Tor, 1993.

Saddam Hussein has sent spies, posing as pseudo-scientists, to Germany to procure a nuclear reactor. One of his men goes on a bloody rampage, raping and murdering women connected with the case. Germany's finest investigator must stop the murders and try to prevent the sale of the nuclear material without an international incident.

L'Amour, Louis. *Last of the Breed.* New York: Bantam, 1986.

A test pilot for experimental aircraft, U.S. Air Force Major Joseph "Joe Mack" Makatozi, part Sioux, part Cheyenne, is forced down over the Bering Sea by Russia. He must seek safety in the uncharted wilds of Siberia, pursued by Russian Intelligence Officer Colonel Azmatev and by a Yakut tracker. He escapes and must use every ounce of his knowledge of the wilds to elude recapture or death in the horrible Siberian winter.

MacLean, Alistair. *Ice Station Zebra.* New York: Crest/Fawcett, 1984.

A British Intelligence agent aboard a nuclear-submarine investigates the mysterious destruction of a meteorological station on the Arctic Ice Cap. He becomes involved in one of the most desperate espionage missions of the Cold War.

Patterson, James. *Along Came a Spider.* New York: Little Brown, 1993.

Alex Cross, a Washington, D.C., homicide detective with a Ph.D. in psychology, and his partner are assigned to the kidnapping of two children of prominent Washington families. Alex becomes romantically involved with Jessie Flanagan, the first woman to become a supervisor of the Secret Service. They keep their romance behind closed doors as they hunt for the kidnapper, Gary Soneji, who knows he is smarter than the police, the Secret Service, and the F.B.I.

Sebastian, Tim. *Saviour's Gate.* New York: Delacorte, 1991.

It is 1990, and Gorbachov decides to defect. Will he get out safely? Will our hero save the luscious Russian double agent? How accurately did the author foreshadow the events of the August putsch? Lots of action and plot twists in this one.

Weber, Janice. *Frost the Fiddler*. New York: St. Martin's, 1992.

Leslie Frost, virtuoso violinist and undercover U.S. agent, witnesses a murder which embroils her in a web of intrigue involving losers, lovers and supercomputers.

Woods, Stuart. *Deep Lie*. New York: Norton, 1986.

A gripping story of the matching of wits of a CIA analyst and a high level KGB spy maker, with the safety of the Western World and Sweden in particular at extreme risk. Much of the story revolves around submarine matters. Of special interest to those readers who enjoy spy stories with marine settings.

———. *White Cargo*. New York: Simon & Schuster, c1988.

While not exactly a "spy novel," this story involves the CIA and does get involved in the "hunt" for a kidnapped girl somewhere in Colombia. Filled with fast-paced, hair-raising airplane maneuvers, really bad "bad guys," jungle sex, and quirky secondary characters, this novel by a respected author is a quick, thrilling read.

Selected Professional References

Barron, Neil. *What Do I Read Next?: A Reader's Guide to Current Genre Fiction.* Detroit: Gale Research, Inc., annual, 1990– .

Biagini, Mary K. *Handbook of Contemporary Fiction for Public Libraries and School Libraries.* Metuchen, NJ: Scarecrow Press, 1989.

Gerhardstein, Virginia Brokaw. *Dickinson's American Historical Fiction.* 5th ed. Metuchen, NJ: Scarecrow Press. 1986.

Gillespie, John Thomas and Corinne J. Naden. *Best Books for Children: Preschool Through Grade 6.* New Providence, NJ: R.R. Bowker, 1990.

Gordon, Lee Diane and Cheryl Tanaka. *World Historical Fiction Guide for Young Adults.* Fort Atkinson, WI: Highsmith Press, 1995.

Helfer, Melinda. *Romance Reader's Handbook.* Brooklyn, NY: Romantic Times, 1989.

Herald, Diana Tixier. *Genreflecting: A Guide to Reading Interests in Genre Fiction.* 4th ed. Englewood, CO: Libraries Unlimited, 1995.

Howard, Elizabeth F. *America As Story: Historical Fiction for Secondary Schools.* Chicago: American Library Association, 1988.

Hubin, Allen J. *Crime Fiction II: A Comprehensive Bibliography.* New York: Garland, 1994.

Husband, Janet and Jonathan F. *Sequels: An Annotated Guide to Novels in Series.* 2nd ed, Chicago: American Library Association, 1990.

Jacob, Merle and Hope Apple. *To Be Continued: An Annotated Guide to Sequels.* Phoenix, AZ: Oryx, 1995.

Lima, Carolyn W. and John A. Lima. *A to Zoo: Subject Access to Children's Picture Books.* New Providence, NJ: R.R. Bowker, 1993.

Mackler, Tasha. *Murder by Category: A Subject Guide to Mystery Fiction.* Metuchen, NJ: Scarecrow Press, 1991.

Menendez, Albert. *Civil War Novels: An Annotated Bibliography.* New York: Garland, 1986.

Norton, Diana R., ed. *The Get Ready Sheet.* Mid-York Library System, Utica, New York, bi-weekly.

Norton, Donna E. *Through the Eyes of a Child: An Introduction to Children's Literature.* New York: Macmillan, 1991.

Radcliffe, Kristin. *Happily Ever After: A Guide to Reading Interests in Romance Fiction.* Englewood, CO: Libraries Unlimited, 1987. OP

Rosenberg, Betty. *Genreflecting: A Guide to Reading Interests in Genre Fiction.* First published in 1982. For latest edition, see listing under Diana Tixier Herald in this bibliography.

Smith, Myron. *War Story Guide: An Annotated Bibliography of Military Fiction.* Metuchen, NJ: Scarecrow Press, 1980.

Vasudevan, Aruna. *Twentieth Century Romance and Historical Writers.* 3rd ed. Detroit, MI: St. James Press, 1994.

Yaakov, Juliette, ed. *Children's Catalog.* New York: H.W. Wilson, 1991.

———— and John Greenfieldt, eds. *Fiction Catalog.* New York: H. W. Wilson, annual.

Contributors

Ted Balcom
Library Administrator,
Villa Park Public Library, Villa Park, Illinois

Merle Jacob
Adult Materials Selection Specialist,
Chicago Public Library, Chicago, Illinois

Sharon Karpiel
Head of Young People's Services,
Elmhurst Public Library, Elmhurst, Illinois

Karen Kaufmann Migaldi
Adult Services Librarian,
Poplar Creek Public Library District, Streamwood, Illinois

Mary Ellen Middleton
Children's Librarian,
Naper Boulevard Branch,
Naperville Public Libraries, Naperville, Illinois

Vivian Mortensen
Head of Reader Services,
Park Ridge Public Library, Park Ridge, Illinois

Georgine N. Olson
Outreach Services Manager,
Fairbanks North Star Borough Public Library and Regional System,
Fairbanks, Alaska

Joyce Saricks
Literature and Audio Services Coordinator,
Downers Grove Public Library, Downers Grove, Illinois

Sally Schuster
Head of Readers' Services,
Addison Public Library, Addison, Illinois

Susan Strunk
Assistant Library Manager,
Naper Boulevard Branch,
Naperville Public Libraries, Naperville, Illinois

Joyce M. Voss
Manager, Community Services,
Arlington Heights Memorial Library, Arlington Heights, Illinois

Debbie Walsh
Head of Adult Services,
Geneva Public Library District, Geneva, Illinois

Debra L. Wordinger
Head of Adult Services,
Indian Prairie Public Library District, Darien, Illinois

Subject Index

Title Index

Note: Pages listed in this index locate book titles listed in the genre bibliographies.

Series Index

Note: Pages listed in this index locate series titles listed in the genre bibliographies.

Author Index

Note: Pages listed in this index locate authors and book titles listed in the genre bibliographies.